# Praise for *Twinsight*

This book is a great read for any multiple birth family member. What a great perspective hearing from twins and their siblings on the dynamics of growing up in a multiple world. A wonderful book for families expecting twins, any family member already experiencing life with twins, and any age adult twins.

—KIM ENGLAND, president of Multiples of America

Throughout my research, I have found that parents of twins know they belong to a very special breed. Dara Lovitz offers a book that these parents will greet with delight. Twinsight highlights the searching questions that inform the daily life of all parents whose children have siblings: love, jealousy, empathy, exclusion, and responsibility. In addition, Lovitz addresses that very special perspective needed when a child has a powerful bond, an intimate identity, and an accompanying need for individuality with a twin.

—TERRI APTER, PhD, author of *The Confident Child: Raising Children to Believe in Themselves*

# TWINSIGHT

FAMILIUS

Copyright © 2018 by Dara Lovitz

Published by Familius LLC, www.familius.com

Familius books are available at special discounts for bulk purchases, whether for sales promotions or for family or corporate use. For more information, contact Familius Sales at 559-876-2170 or email orders@familius.com.

Library of Congress Cataloging-in-Publication Data
2017958505

Print ISBN 9781945547720
Ebook ISBN 9781641700221

Printed in the United States of America

Edited by DeAnna Acker
Cover design by David Miles
Book design by Brooke Jorden

10 9 8 7 6 5 4 3 2 1

First Edition

# TWINSIGHT

## A Guide to Raising Emotionally Healthy Twins

with Advice from the Experts (Academics)
and the REAL Experts (Twins)

### DARA LOVITZ

*Dedicated to all of the individuals I interviewed.*
  *You opened up to me.*
  *You shared with me your insights.*
  *You entrusted me with your special memories.*
  *I am forever grateful to you.*
  *Without you, there would be no book.*
  *Thank you.*


*Also dedicated to my beloved husband, Josh, and our amazing twin daughters Eden and Tal.*
  *It is even more so the case that without you, there would be no book.*

# Contents

# Foreword

**M**y identical twin sister and I attended the Twins Days Festival in Twinsburg, Ohio—the largest annual gathering of twins in the world—in August of 2016 for the first time ever. Over 1,800 twins registered that year to celebrate their unique status as a twin, whether they were fraternal or identical. Twins of all ages dressed alike, from head to toe, sending the message that they embraced being "the twins," or being treated as a unit rather than two individuals with different interests and personalities. My twin sister and I were there conducting interviews with identical twins for my most recent research project on identical twins. As a family sociologist, backed with the experience of being an identical twin, I thought I had little to learn about identical twins—but I was wrong. Based on the stories told by the participants in my study, there are certainly some twins who embrace their twin status and have not been affected negatively, but there are some twins who report that being a twin presents a number of challenges, including striving for individuality,

dealing with comparisons to their twin, and difficulty with relationships, including friendships, romantic relationships, and
sibling relationships. *Twinsight*, written by Dara Lovitz, mother
of fraternal twin daughters, is a book that serves as an essential
guide to parents of twins (and other multiples). Readers will learn
about the unique relationship shared by twins, but most importantly, this book is written for parents and caregivers of twins, so
that they can learn how to raise emotionally healthy and confident twins.

According to the 2015 National Vital Statistics Report based
on data from 2014, the twin birth rate was 33.9 twins per 1,000 in
2014, the highest ever reported.[1] The likelihood of having *identical* twins, which happens when one fertilized egg divides in half,
is holding steady at about 3 to 5 in 1000 births.[2] With the increase
in the twinning rate in the past few decades, due mostly to an
increase in the use of fertility drugs as well as advanced maternal
age, the experience of parenting twins (and other multiples) has
become more common than prior to the 1980s. Thus, *Twinsight*
is a must have for parents who find themselves preparing for the
arrival of twins as well as for those who are in the midst of raising
twins.

I was contacted by author Dara Lovitz after she listened to
my NPR radio interview that aired on WHYY-FM in September
2016. She was interested in my research on identical twins and
wanted to meet to discuss ways in which our research overlapped.
After our first conversation, I realized that our research shared
both similarities and differences. The main difference, of course,
is that she is writing from the perspective of a parent of fraternal
twins. I, on the other hand, am an identical twin who has recently
completed research about identical twins. However, in order to
learn about the experience of being raised as an identical twin, we
both went directly to the source—twins themselves (and siblings

of twins, in Dara's case). Lovitz's research complements my own in that the goal of her research is to provide advice on how to raise emotionally healthy twins while my research takes a retrospective look at identical twins, telling their stories.

While there are a number of books on raising multiples, Dara Lovitz's *Twinsight* is unique in a number of ways. First, she interviewed more than eighty twins (even some triplets), asking them what they liked and did not like about the way they were raised. She also took it one step further by interviewing singleton siblings of twins to find out if and how they were affected by being raised in a family with twins. Last, she consulted with educators and psychologists to gain a diversity of perspectives on the rearing of twins. Complementing the data gathered from interviews and consultations with professionals is her own personal experience as the mother of fraternal twins—an interesting and thorough combination.

In *Twinsight*, advice is provided on how to encourage individuality, whether it is in terms of personality traits or friendships. Lovitz even suggests holding separate birthday parties or asking for non-shared birthday gifts for the twins. Lovitz also highlights a topic not often discussed by twins—the caretaking bond—and the sacrifices often made by one twin for the other. Based on stories from her interviews with twins, Lovitz provides suggestions on how to relieve the caretaking bond. Throughout the book, Lovitz makes the case that one-on-one time is essential for raising emotionally healthy twins. On a related note, it is also important for parents and caregivers to assure that other singleton siblings are receiving similar one-on-one time, especially since there is research that shows that relationships with non-twin siblings are generally not as close as the twin-sibling relationship. Another important theme that came out of Lovitz's research is the insistence that twins not be compared—by parents, siblings, relatives, friends, and others. Lovitz also presents a question that the majority of parents will have to face at some point: should parents separate twins in school? In addition, Lovitz provides advice on how to best prepare twins for other relationships, including friendships and romantic/intimate relationships. In the final chapter, Lovitz encourages parents to validate their children's feelings—to really take the time to think about what it is like to be an identical twin, with all of the benefits and downfalls.

As a parent of two little boys born thirteen months apart, I certainly reflect on the way my parents raised my twin sister and me. There are some things that I emulate—such as instilling strong family values in my children—and others that I avoid, such as the use of physical discipline. Although my parents loved the fact that we were twins and, in my opinion, did a fine job of raising us, there are inevitable "costs" associated with being a twin, such as shared birthday parties and unintentional comparisons to the other twin. Perhaps some parents are better prepared than others to raise emotionally healthy twins and multiples, but who couldn't use a tip or two? To be fair, the choices my mother and father made—such as shared birthday presents, referring to us as "the girls" or "the twins," and dressing us alike until we started to resist in about the third grade—were made with good intentions. They did not think that there was anything wrong with their choices, and back in the early 1980s when my twin sister and I were in elementary school, there were very few books on how to raise multiples, let alone parenting books on raising emotionally healthy children. Times have changed, and I believe parents are now more inclined to read about the dos and don'ts of raising children—even though family time is more pressed than ever with a majority of families attempting the balancing act between work and family life. Even though my parents did a fine job in raising us kids—making sure to treat us equally and never showing favoritism—I strongly believe that my parents would have benefited from the knowledge and advice shared by Lovitz in *Twinsight*. I view it as an essential guide for parents who want emotionally healthy and confident twins. In short, *Twinsight* is an extraordinary book, written with great care, especially when it comes to incorporating the multiple perspectives of twins themselves, singleton siblings, and professionals as well as Lovitz's own voice/perspective as a parent of twins. I urge parents and caregivers of twins to seriously consider her advice in *Twinsight*.

Joleen Loucks Greenwood, PhD
Associate Professor of Sociology,
Kutztown University of Pennsylvania

1. Brady Hamilton et al. and the National Center for Health Statistics, "Births: Final Data for 2014," *National Vital Statistics Reports* 64, no. 12 (December 23, 2015): 2, https://www.cdc.gov/nchs/data/nvsr/nvsr64/nvsr64_12.pdf.

2. BabyCenter Medical Advisory Board, "Your Likelihood of Having Twins or More," BabyCenter.com, last updated January 2016, https://www.babycenter.com/0_your-likelihood-of-having-twins-or-more_3575.bc#articlesection1.

# Introduction

## Two Tiny Heartbeats, Too Many Questions

I didn't notice them right away, but when the doctor pointed to the two tiny, pulsing heartbeats on the ultrasound monitor, I lost my breath. Tears instantly welled up in my eyes. The joy of becoming pregnant would have been enough, but now I had a double joy on the horizon.

As with many times in my life, though, great joy came with great worry. *Two children? Can I physically sustain both of them? How will their individual presences affect each other? Will the delivery be premature? Will I have to deliver by Caesarean section? Will they spend time in the neonatal intensive care unit?*

As I answered each of those questions, plenty more concerns occupied the anxiety center in my brain: *Will I be able to care for both of them? How will I breastfeed them? What if they don't sleep on the same schedule? Will I be able to sleep at all? Ever?*

And then: *Will they be best friends? Will they hate each other? Will they look alike? Will they dress alike? How will they differ? How will they be the same?*

The most important question I asked myself, however, was this: *What can I do to help them develop in an emotionally healthy way?*

Answering that question seemed imperative to me. I recognized soon after they were born that only rarely did either of them enjoy one hundred percent of my attention. I was constantly juggling both of their needs, and I was seldom giving undivided attention to any one child for an extended period of time. This division of focus differed drastically from the newborn- and toddler-raising experiences of my peers who had singletons.

Simple activities, like taking a child to the supermarket, the playground, or a restaurant, were significantly more difficult with two infants instead of one. A parent of twin infants must employ the use of a double sling, a double stroller, or a combination of a single baby sling and a shopping cart at any given time. A parent of twin infants will occasionally have to leave one baby in the car (usually crying) while running the other baby into the house and placing him into a bouncy seat. A parent of twins can try a trip to the playground but will likely be confronted with an emergency conflict that requires weighing one disastrous outcome with another. If both children are on opposite sides of the equipment, for example, do you go to the one at the top of the very high slide or the one climbing up the rope ladder with rungs situated too far apart? A parent of twin toddlers will generally not be able to take both children to a restaurant for a meal unless at least one child is napping in the stroller. A parent of twins can rarely enjoy one-on-one story time accompanied by individualized cuddling.

Parents of twins simply cannot give their children the same quantity of attention that their singleton-parent peers give their children. But surely quality should be more important than quantity, and surely it is possible to give one's twin children the quality attention they deserve . . . right?

It thus became my quest to learn how I could be the best possible parent to my twin children so they didn't feel denied parental love, attention, and affection because of the mere circumstance of their births.

Researching how to raise emotionally healthy twins has taught me a lot and opened my eyes to the dangers of my misguided instincts. Parenting twins, it turns out, is not intuitive. At least not for me.

I never had the so-called "mommy gene" that so many of my friends seemed to possess. When I was a married woman without kids in my late twenties, I was amazed at the starry-eyed looks my girlfriends had in their eyes when they talked about being a mother one day. Or how we could be walking down the street having an adult conversation when suddenly, and without warning, my friend would dart across the street without regard for the oncoming cars and approach a stranger walking with a baby in a stroller.

There was a point when I almost didn't want to be around all of these girls with the names of their nonexistent babies already picked out, because I just wasn't there yet. I just didn't have "it"— the mommy gene—and I secretly worried that not having that gene meant that whenever I did decide to have kids, I would be a terrible mom.

I remember a Jim Gaffigan bit about his insecurity in being a parent. He said, "Every night before I get my one hour of sleep, I have the same thought: *Well, that's a wrap on another day of acting like I know what I'm doing.* I wish I were exaggerating, but I'm not. Most of the time, I feel entirely unqualified to be a parent. I call these times 'being awake.'" I found this as humorous as it was terrifying. If Jim Gaffigan, father of five, didn't feel qualified to be a parent, how could I possibly meet the minimum standards?

And, if I'm being honest, I'm not really the type to settle for the bare minimum of anything. Except house cleaning. I loathe vacuuming, counter wiping, floor sweeping, and toy organizing so much that I will do literally the least one can do in each of these categories. But in most other things, I like to do way more than the minimum—I like to excel. So as a parent, I want the gold star. I want to raise my kids to be compassionate, driven, happy, intelligent, kind, and thoughtful. I want them to be wonderful people at every stage of their growth. How do I help them in their development?

## My Methodology

My many questions led me to this personal quest: learn how to be the best parent of twins that I can be. (My kids deserve no less!) That quest led me to perform countless hours of research and eventually write this book.

I focused my research on the emotional health of our twin children. It's easy to find books on potty-training twins, or "surviving the first year," or even traveling with them. It's not so easy to find a book that goes beyond the logistical difficulties inherent in having two needy infants and into the psychological impact of being a twin, or how parents can cultivate the emotional health of their twins. So I interviewed twins* and triplets as well as their non-multiples siblings.

*Note that while I usually refer to "twins," most of the information in this guidebook would be helpful for parents of other multiple sets as well.

To date, I have interviewed more than eighty individuals. I purposely did not interview twins together; I wanted their answers to be honest and unfettered. And I promised confidentiality. I didn't want interviewees to silence themselves in any way out of fear of their twin sibling hearing the information. To ensure total confidentiality, I have changed names and, in some cases, genders and other identifying information in the anecdotes that I feature in the book. Many stories that twins told me were echoed by others I interviewed who had the same experiences. I have intentionally only included stories that cannot be ascribed to a particular interviewee in order to protect everyone's privacy.

Some interviews were in person, but, in the interest of diversity, many interviews took place across time zones and over the phone. The youngest interviewee was in her twenties, and the oldest interviewee was in his eighties. There was a broad range of ethnicity, race, religion, socioeconomic class, and education among my interviewees. I asked these wonderfully open individuals about what worked and what didn't work for them in their upbringing and how their twinship has affected their adulthoods. They told me their stories. They shared their insights.

I also interviewed adults who grew up as the non-twin (or "singleton") sibling of twins. I wanted to hear their impressions of the relationship between their twin siblings, the relationship between the pair of twins and the parents, and their own relationship with the twin siblings and the parents. I wanted to hear the positive and negative aspects of being raised in a family with twin siblings.

Many of the twins and singleton siblings of twins I interviewed told me that I should talk to their parents because they believed their parents did a great job raising them. Yet parents are the one group I purposely avoided. I wanted this advice to come as the result of talking with twins and their siblings themselves. I anticipated the answer to my question *How do I raise emotionally healthy twins?* would be different if I asked actual twins themselves rather than the parents of twins. Indeed, much of the advice that I compiled as the result of conversations with the twins has differed from the general advice I see in books and articles written by parents of twins. Apparently, raising twins is not intuitive for others either.

I also felt, to the extent that the answers coming from twins themselves were different, the compiled advice would be more effective for parents than other advice guides on the market. This advice comes firsthand. It is not from individuals who raised twins but rather from those who experienced being raised as twins.

I believe that in order for parents to be effective, they must frequently put themselves in the shoes of their children. They must ask, *How does my child see the world? How is my child experiencing this moment? How does my child perceive my actions?* So I approached this writing with the goal of allowing parents to see the world from their twin children's viewpoints. I want twins to feel heard. I hope that by composing tips and advice with their voices guiding me, I can bring parents closer to truly understanding their children.

After I interviewed the adult twins, I consulted professionals in psychology and education. I wanted to hear how their professional advice supported or, in some cases, conflicted with my results from talking to the twins themselves.

Each chapter contains information from the twin interviewees as well as from professionals. I conclude each chapter with a list of tips that I hope readers will find helpful.

I purposely wrote this book in a way that would appeal to the many different faces of parenting. I excluded any presumption that a family contains only one mother and one father. Unless there was a gender-specific concept (like breastfeeding), I kept references to the targeted audience gender-neutral (e.g., "parent" versus "mother"),* and I tried to include anecdotes that would be particularly meaningful to fathers.

*So as not to use the historical default of "he," "him," and "his" as the subject pronoun, I will intentionally alternate between "he/him/his" and "she/her/hers" in the most balanced way possible.

As the comedian Jay Mohr explains in his book *No Wonder My Parents Drank: Tales from a Stand-Up Dad*, gone are the days when dads avoid child-rearing in most forms. When Mohr was growing up, fathers almost never took their kids to parks. "If someone's father was at the park, it usually meant someone was in trouble."[1] Now, though, dads are at the park, the playground, the preschool open house, and the dress-shopping excursion.

In my writing, I was also intentionally mindful that some families have fewer than or more than two parental figures. I often use the term "caregiver" to signify those varied individuals who might be responsible for the children's emotional well-being: biological parents, adoptive parents, grandparents, babysitters, nannies, and other family members and relations.

In my investigation, I occasionally came across research which contained conclusions based on data documenting animal studies. Most scientists agree that nonhuman animals are not sufficiently accurate predictors of outcomes in humans. Thus, I did not rely upon animal studies. When I refer to research, the reader may safely assume that I am referring to research that used human subjects.

Occasionally, I'll refer to "monozygotic" or "dizygotic" twins. Monozygotic twins result from the fertilization of one sperm and one egg. The fertilized egg then splits mere days after the initial fertilization. The two zygotes usually share the same chromosomes and placenta. Monozygotic twins are referred to in layperson terms as "identical twins." Dizygotic twins result from the fertilization of two different eggs with two different sperms. These zygotes do not share the same chromosomes and do not share the same placenta. Dizygotic twins are referred to in layperson terms as "fraternal twins."

# The History of Family

The pressure modern parents place on themselves is undeniable. Yet it wasn't always that way. The history of families is fascinating. For more years than not, one's children were one's commodities. Jennifer Senior, in *All Joy and No Fun: The Paradox of Modern Parenting*, explains:

> It wasn't until our soldiers returned from World War II that childhood, as we now know it, began. The family economy was no longer built on a system of reciprocity, with parents sheltering and feeding their children, and children, in return, kicking something back into the family till. The relationship became asymmetrical. Children stopped working, and parents worked twice as hard. Children went from being our employees to our bosses.[2]

As the sociologist Viviana Zelizer noted in *Pricing the Priceless Child: The Changing Social Value of Children*, children went from being "economically worthless" to "emotionally priceless."[3] Indeed, we modern parents invest a lot of time and intellect into the psychological well-being of our children. We give time-outs—or don't. We co-sleep with our children—or don't. We praise our children's achievements—or don't. However we do it, the psychological impact of our actions and words drives our parenting endeavors.

# Twins across Cultures

Twins are so interesting that every culture has a differ-ent way of confronting their mystique. Even today, some countries view twins as bad luck, causing parents to abandon their newborns.

The Yoruba of Nigeria today happen to have the largest dizygotic twinning rate in the world—three percent of all births, which is more than double the rate of the rest of the world.

Twins were seen as complementary in the case of Greek myth-ological twins Apollo and Artemis; Apollo was the god of the sun, and Artemis was associated with the moon. Similarly, the Xingu people of Brazil had stories of twins who occupied the sun and the moon, respectively.

Greek mythology also highlighted the partnership and close relationship of twins in the case of Castor and Pollux, who were inseparable teammates and friends. When Castor was killed, Pollux asked Zeus to allow him to share his immortality with Castor so they could be kept together. They were converted into the constellation Gemini.

This kind of complementary partnership is also seen in ancient India, where the Ashvins ("horsemen") were twins representing the sunrise and sunset. They were personifications of the early dawn that chased away the darkness and drove out evil.

African mythology has varying interpretations of twinships. The Dogon tribe of Mali, for instance, regards twinship as com-pletion and perfection. The Nummo (or Nommo) consists of multiple sets of twins and is considered the key spiritual collective figure of the Dogon.

The Yoruba people of Nigeria historically believed that twins were evil and, in some cases, would kill one or both twins, and possibly the mother. In modern times, twins are generally seen by the Yoruba as a gift from God, a sign of good fortune, and are celebrated. However, they may also view twins as having the power to bring upon misfortune, disease, or death. For those reasons, twin Yoruba children typically enjoy a more permissive upbringing than that experienced by their singleton peers.

In Nuer culture in Sudan, twins were considered to carry the closest possible human relationship and were often perceived as one person. Twins were considered children of god, akin to birds whose spirits soared in the sky. Upon the death of infant twins, the babies were placed in a reed basket that was positioned in a tree so they could fly away. Upon the death of an adult twin, the Nuer would build a platform on which the body was placed and covered with a hide. Typically, other Nuer bodies would be buried in the earth immediately, but twins, holding a superhuman status, were elevated in this way to distinguish them from others.

In West Africa and Haiti, twins were exalted as supernatural beings whom the people revered and feared.

In Korean culture, twins were typically considered bad luck and separated at birth.

In Aztec mythology, the twin deity Xolotl was the god of fire, lightning, sickness, and deformity. The birth of twins was greeted with horror and fear. Aztecs would often kill at least one of the twins.

Currently, in Madagascar, twin babies are traditionally abandoned by their mothers because they are seen as a curse that brings bad luck to their family. In the past, they were left out in nature to die. In modern times, they are placed in orphanages or adoption centers. Families who decide to keep their twins are banished from their villages and have to live in makeshift tents on the outskirts of their former communities. Most landlords will not rent homes to them because of the perceived bad luck the twins will bring.

Today in the United States, we are marveled by twins. We study their bond. We enjoy stories of twins reunited after years apart and who married women with the same first name. We have examples of twins in pop culture: Marge Simpson's twin sisters, who smoke, have the same voice, and live together; the mischievous twin sisters in the movie *The Parent Trap*, who plot to reunite their divorced parents; and the Winklevoss twins, whose story and Facebook lawsuit became well known in the movie *The Social Network*. We watch viral videos of twin infants in high chairs rocking back and forth in unison to the sound of their father's guitar and twin toddlers talking to each other in a language only they understand. We have national conferences to discuss the results of twin studies. We have a multi-day festival for twins from around the world to gather, enjoy live entertainment, take photos, and admire fellow multiples in matching outfits. Even I, as a parent of twins who makes a conscious effort not to overemphasize the novelty of twins, get excited when I see two children who look identical to each other in age, size, and appearance. Apparently, I am not immune to the charms identical children emanate to the rest of the world.

## Twins in Science

The rate of twins is on the rise due to increased use of fertility treatments, as well as the general trend toward a more advanced maternal age in childbirth.

Twins are seen as a boon to researchers who can study epigenetics, nature versus nurture, and epidemiologic conundrums by using both twin siblings in their studies. Twins, like other biologically related siblings, share genes in common. Such genetic similarity may result in other resemblances. Multiple studies have shown there is a genetic component to social attitudes, such as

attitudes toward physical activities, intelligence, aesthetic appearance, and leadership behaviors. Academic achievement and, in
particular, verbal ability are partly heritable. There is also a genetic
influence on political attitudes (although notably **not** party affil-
iation). Attitudes toward nuclear power, organized religion,
global warming, property taxes, the death penalty, euthanasia,
and other political and world viewpoints as well as sensitivity to
(or animosity toward) other cultural groups are all substantially
influenced by genetics. Scientists will continue to research the
biological pathways that are responsible for this finding. And as
you can imagine, the conclusion confounds political strategists
who loathe information that suggests that there is an element to
social persuasion that is beyond their control.

Twins also have lower rates of suicide. There are multiple
explanations for this, but one prevailing concept is that twins
generally have stronger family ties. Closeness with at least one
other family member as the reasoning behind twins' relatively
lower suicide rate makes sense when one considers that the more
socially connected one is, the better his mental health. In fact,
whether a twin or not, longevity in older people is correlated to
the rate at which they remain socially connected to other people.
In other words, the less isolated older people are, the more likely
they are to outlive their less social peers.

## A Focus on Emotions

While there are a few fun facts highlighting the differences
between twins and non-twins (e.g., twins are more likely be left
handed!), in general terms, twins are not very different from non-
twins. Studies examining psychopathology between twins and
non-twins have typically concluded that there is no significant
difference between the population of twins and the population at

large. Studies involving lifestyle characteristics, personality traits, behavioral problems, depression, anxiety, and severe psychotic disorders indicate that twins demonstrate no higher incidence than the population at large.

What *is* generally different between twins and non-twins is how they develop emotionally, given the unique circumstances of their births. Sharing the same birthday, parents, and siblings, as well as many formative life experiences, render the emotional makeup and personality of twins distinctive from non-twins. Growing up as a twin is not the same as growing up as a singleton. I seek to highlight those differences. And it is those differences that challenge the preconceived notions that parents of twins have—raising a twin child is not the same as raising a singleton child.

There is a Jewish proverb that I love. It says, "A mother understands what a child does not say." At the risk of being audacious (after all, who am I to edit a proverb?), I would change it to say, "A *loving and empathic parent* understands what a child does not say." Your child will not tell you explicitly every time he is hurt by your words, your actions, or your omissions. After a long day of school, your child will not always explain how he felt when his twin teamed up with a mutual friend against him, or when a girl he liked called him by his twin's name, or when, at lunch, the Spanish teacher questioned why he is not as proficient in the language as his twin. Your singleton will not describe how it makes her feel to see twice as many framed photos of her twin siblings hanging in the house compared to the number of photos of her.

Your child will not always speak. But you need to always listen—to what he's saying and to what he is not saying. I hope this book helps.

1. Jay Mohr, *No Wonder My Parents Drank: Tales from a Stand-Up Dad* (New York: Simon & Schuster, 2010), 6–7.

2. Jennifer Senior, *All Joy and No Fun: The Paradox of Modern Parenthood* (New York: Ecco, 2015), 9.

3. Viviana Zelizer, *Pricing the Priceless Child: The Changing Social Value of Children* (Princeton, NJ: Basic Books, 1985), 57.

# CHAPTER ONE

# Unique Companionship

*I am never alone.*

—Arnold

At the risk of stating the obvious, twins share a unique companionship that is unlike any other. Twins have someone with whom they share practically every life experience. They are growing up at the same time—engaging with the same peers, confronting the same issues, and navigating the same challenges. Even in adult twins I interviewed whose relationship is currently strained or dissolved, there was still a recognition that, at least as children, their twinship bond was strong and their relationship was unlike any other.

I interviewed enough twins to examine their bond in many contexts, and I found some common themes among the adult twins I interviewed.

# Built-In Playmates

When my twins were newborns, other twin parents would accurately assure me that while parenting twins is more challenging than parenting a singleton in the beginning, it would not always be so. Indeed, when the twins reach two to three years of age, a twin parent has it easier because there's a built-in playmate for one's child. The parent need not scramble every day to provide endless entertainment or schedule playdates outside the home. The parent of twins can rely on the twins themselves to provide company and entertainment to each other.

From the twin children's perspective, this is generally perceived as a positive thing as well. For twins who lived in provincial areas, "where your next-door neighbor's house was miles away," they were grateful that they had a playmate their own age at home. As one interviewee put it, "My twin sister helped distract me from the monotony of rural living." For a twin interviewee who grew up in a "rough neighborhood" in the city, she was grateful she had her twin brother to walk to and from school with every day. All of the twin or triplet interviewees commented that they appreciated that at nearly every hour of the day, they had a buddy to play with and talk to. They had someone who was experiencing life at the same pace—someone to "teach me how to braid my Barbie's hair" or "ride bikes with me after school." They never felt alone.

Of course, as twins age, this perk can become more of a burden. Around the later elementary school years, some individuals would have preferred a different playmate once in a while. Humans tend to crave variety, and companionship is no exception. Desiring a different playmate does not necessarily signify a rift in the twins' friendship. In fact, as the saying goes, absence makes the heart grow fonder, and some time apart can help the twin children appreciate and show more love to each other.

By the time they were two years old, my not-yet-verbal twins were adept at communicating that they needed time apart. For instance, Tal—who was usually very even tempered and kind—would hit her sister on the head. Not hard, but enough to shock Eden into crying. What could bring my docile and well-mannered Tal to resort to hitting her sister? Simply frustration at her constant presence. Tal hitting Eden was a sign that they needed time apart, and when I delivered said antidote—even just separate activities on different sides of the room—they would return to each other amicably and peacefully. (I was secretly tickled by this act of aggression. I loved imagining the slapstick nature of the act applied to adult situations. Picture it: You're at a dinner party, and some-one you just met is droning on and on about a topic you detest . . . and BONK! You whack him on the head out of nowhere, and he gets the message—you'd like to be alone now. I'm embarrassed to admit that this isn't the only instance in which I wished the rules for acceptable behavior for toddlers could apply to adults as well—conspicuous nose-picking, for example.)

I'm glad that my children at least sometimes made it clear that they needed time apart. It was a nice reminder that after spend-ing so much effort trying to satisfy their physical survival needs (clothing, diaper changes, food, sleep), I should not neglect their emotional survival needs either.

I'm not alone here; I think parents often become a little com-placent about—and therefore dependent on—the automatic and unscheduled twin sibling playdate. While it's convenient to have that built-in playmate under your roof, a parent would do well to expand the social circle and schedule some playdates with outside friends. (Of course, on a snowy day when you don't feel like shoveling the driveway, a parent of twins is certainly entitled to take advantage of the built-in playdate and celebrate family within the cozy home!)

However often your twins play together or apart, it is clear that, as young children, at least, they enjoy a great advantage over their singleton peers.

# Proverbial Hand-Holders

There are many "firsts" in a person's life. Some of the firsts that greatly affect a young child are the first day of daycare or preschool, the first time being left alone with a babysitter, the first time stepping foot in the ocean or pool, and the first time in a public crowd. Imagine how intimidating these vastly new experiences could be for a child who is still mastering some foundational milestones like communication and motor skills. Now imagine that same child having a family member, a peer, who will be there at the same time, experiencing the same thing.

There's comfort inherent in the multiples scenario. When faced with a daunting new experience, each child can look no further than the car seat next to her, or the little chair at the same table, to see a familiar (and most likely comforting) face. Twin interviewees recalled going to overnight camp, or going to a new and very big high school building, as moments when they were thankful they had their twin nearby. As one interviewee explained, "Nothing was as scary for me as it was for other kids going through the same thing because my brother was there, experiencing the same thing with me."

For twins Rebecca and Ellen, Rebecca was "the braver one." Ellen reported that "Rebecca had no fear and would always try things first." Whether they were swimming in a lake on their first day of camp or roller skating in the middle school parking lot, Ellen would watch Rebecca try the activity and, upon seeing that Rebecca was safe, Ellen would try it.

Twins tend to be each other's transitional object. A transitional object, typically a soft blanket or a stuffed animal (often called a "lovey"), is used to comfort a young child during a time of transition in her life. A transitional object helps soothe a child when a parent or familiar caregiver is unavailable. One's twin can provide the familiarity and comfort that an inanimate transitional object would otherwise offer. As we will discuss in Chapter Two, twins who use each other as transitional objects have a harder time separating from one another and developing their own senses of identity and individuality.

Even though it can be seen as a setback to an individual's emotional growth and independence, most twins will say that having someone by their side during life's challenges is one of the greatest perks of being a twin.

## Caretakers

Twin children and young adults frequently assume the role of caretaker for one another. Sometimes the individual has an innate desire to care for others, and that person's twin sibling presents the first opportunity to do so. Sometimes twins become each other's caretaker when their parents are otherwise unavailable. Caretaking in the younger years could involve trying to help change the diaper of a co-twin (as my twins did when they were two years old) or wiping the co-twin's nose with a tissue. As the children age, caretaking could be preparing food for a co-twin, styling hair, or bringing medicine to the ill sibling.

One adult twin I interviewed described how her sister flushed her drugs down the toilet in college, while another relayed a story about her brother deriding her for not living up to her potential professionally. The adult multiples I interviewed engaged in all sorts of caretaker activities, like physically defending a teenage brother who was being beaten by the neighborhood bully or allowing a twenty-eight-year-old brother to move in with him so he could heal from a painful breakup.

The vast majority of twins with whom I spoke all felt instinctively defensive of their twin siblings. Many were able to recall specific instances where someone was insulting or bullying their twin and they stepped in to defend, fight back, or find some way to safely extract the victimized twin from the situation. I have been told that they have no tolerance for others insulting their twin siblings. As one put it, "If you have a problem with my sister, just don't tell me about it, because I will never take your side," while another said, "If you mess with [my twin sibling], you mess with me."

Twins Harmony and Trisha were middle children in a family of nine. Their older sister Marilyn commented that she could never "gossip" with either twin about the other. "They were willing to talk behind the backs of any other family member, but not each other," she said. "Even if what I was saying about Trisha came from a good place, like when I was worried about her drinking behavior, Harmony would defend her and then say, 'Well, if that is true—and I'm not saying it is—then how can we help her?'"

Generally, the propensity for caretaking among twins was reciprocal. Many of those who took care of their siblings in one way or another explained that they enjoyed the comfort of knowing that their twin, in turn, always "had their back." But there were also twin interviewees who felt that the caretaking in their twinship was unilateral. Twin interviewee Josephine, for instance, felt "more like an older sister" than a twin. This was particularly the case when they went to different colleges and her sister, Robin, would often call her crying, seeking comfort for practically any negative occurrence. "Once I saw that it was Robin calling, I would always immediately pick up the phone, which annoyed the hell out of my boyfriend," Josephine said. "He told me I was enabling Robin, which really upset me and caused a fight between us. But ultimately I think he was right; Robin and I had a tight bond, but it wasn't healthy."

In Chapter Three, there will be a larger discussion of the unhealthy emotional imbalance that results from one twin constantly feeling responsible for the other twin. For many twins, though, the phenomenon just resulted in honing caretaking skills sooner than their singleton peers.

## Teammates

Other twin interviewees communicated about their relationship using sports terms, like *coach* and *teammate*. Some of the twins played coach by helping their siblings achieve specific goals. For example, in the younger years, they helped a sibling communicate with words instead of acting out or, in the older years, they helped a sibling improve interviewing techniques for jobs. There was the twin who described holding a kitchen stool when she was four years old so her co-twin could grab the cookies on the counter. There was also a poignant recollection of someone who was on the same tennis team as her twin. She purposely lost a match so that she would not be paired against her twin in the next round.

Twins typically report that their twin sibling understands them better than anyone else, including their parents. They will generally rely on their twin's introspect and advice over that of another individual. It may take years of being with a significant other before twins feel as emotionally close with their partner as they feel with their twin sibling. Some adult twins reported that they would still go to their twin sibling first for advice before going to a parent or spouse. In Chapter Eight, I explore the conflict between the close twin relationship and a less close relationship with a romantic partner. Indeed, the depth of synchrony between twins creates a bond that is unlike any other.

## Emotional Dependence

Twin relationships could also result in emotional dependency. For instance, twin interviewees Greta and Bill were emotionally dependent on one another. When their father died, it was comforting for them to have each other during the grieving process. Greta said she and Bill had a similar relationship with their father. They enjoyed riding in their father's car around the neighborhood and recalled fondly when he took them to the arena to watch a professional basketball game. When their father died, they seemed to grieve in the same way at the same time, and thus, as Greta explained, "My brother understood better than anyone else the pain I was suffering." Greta felt that having her twin brother by her side helped her find strength in this otherwise emotionally traumatizing experience.

Many twins also described divorce as a painful, traumatic event made survivable by the presence of a co-twin who understood the level of upset and suffering. Jeffrey Kluger, author of *The Sibling Effect: What the Bonds among Brothers and Sisters Reveal about Us*, explains that some people experience a crisis and want nothing to do with the people with whom they experienced it simply because being around those people conjures up painful thoughts. Yet others—and, I would argue, particularly twin siblings—"who make it out of the familial foxhole alive will react completely differently—developing a deep and indelible love for the people who survived with them, one that is stronger than it was before the shooting started."[1]

A twin with a close bond to his co-twin tends to absorb the emotions of the co-twin. Even when the stimulus affects only one twin, his co-twin often feels the joy or pain as though he were experiencing it himself firsthand. Twin interviewees reported to me various instances in which they felt like they were suffering at practically the same level as their co-twin when the co-twin was experiencing the event alone. Whether it's a bad grade, rejection from university, or loss of employment, a twin tends to feel and, in some cases, echo his twin's emotional response.

When my family was at a friend's house for dinner, four-year old Tal fell off a heavy dining room chair that, in turn, fell on top of her. My husband rushed to pick up the screaming child and carried her to the next room to comfort her. I stayed at the table and I noticed Eden bowing her head. When I asked her what was wrong, she ran around the table to where I was sitting, climbed onto my lap, and buried her head in my neck as she wept. It wasn't until Tal emerged seemingly injury-free from the other room that Eden was able to stop crying.

Thankfully, this shared response also manifests with emotions on the other end of the spectrum; twins share in joyous occasions as well. Twins have reported various moments of empathic elation: the twin who felt personally victorious when a co-twin was accepted into a prestigious summer program, the twin who experienced breathless exhilaration watching her co-twin bungee jump, and the twin who cried tears of joy when his co-twin delivered her first child. One triplet interviewee poignantly described a sibling's individual success as "happiness times three."

But emotional dependency could be a sign of an unhealthy relationship. In one instance, a woman's twin brother was so emotionally dependent on her that when she moved away from their country to live in America when she was twenty-seven years old, her brother was so deeply affected by this "loss" that he ignored her for two years. He had felt that she abandoned him, and even though they have reconciled in part, their relationship has never fully recuperated.

I also interviewed female twins who were always put in separate classrooms at first, but then one of the sisters would become so emotionally distraught that they always ended up back in the same class. This pattern continued all through elementary and middle schools. For the sister who was not distraught at the separation, she "never got to enjoy" the experience of being her own person in school.

As we will discuss in Chapters Two and Three, codependence can be unhealthy and detrimental to a person's development of identity, independence, and self.

## Social Issues

Twins can take great comfort in having a built-in playmate and friend. But there are negative social outcomes that can result. Arnold and Drew are a perfect example of the positive and negative outcomes of having your best friend with you at all times.

They were in the same classes at school and even chose to attend the same college, where they were roommates all four years. Arnold recalled, "It was great having Drew by my side with every transition in life. If moving away from home to go to college could be less scary because my brother was with me, why wouldn't I want that?" Arnold said that he always felt part of a special club that had a special language and special memories and that no one else could join. Now, in their sixties, they still communicate every day and have a close bond.

But, in looking back at his childhood, he wonders if his parents should have intervened at times to prevent them from living in their own twin-protected bubble. "We would go to parties," Arnold reported, "and we'd just go to one side of the room and talk to each other the whole time. Our parents maybe shouldn't have let us drift away into our own world that no one else could relate to. Maybe they should have forced us to go socialize with others at the party—relatives and friends and whatnot. If they wanted us to have any social graces later in life, they should have pushed us to go and talk to others."

I interviewed identical twins Perry and Jonah in separate interviews, and they both complained that they had difficulty making friends in high school. Perry reported, "High school was hard because people couldn't differentiate us so they wouldn't really talk about anything important. Like, if I was talking to someone, it was obvious that he didn't know if he was talking to me or my brother. So the conversation didn't go anywhere because he didn't want to repeat something he already said to me—or reference something he had said to my brother."

Jonah, in his own interview, concurred. "High school was the hardest time for me because I couldn't make real friends. All the conversations seemed superficial, I think because people didn't know for sure whether I was Perry or me. No one talked with me about anything too deep, so I didn't bond with anyone."

Of course, a non-twin can become socially dependent upon a good friend, but this is a much more prevalent problem among twins because, unlike friends who come in and out of one's life, a twin is there from the beginning and usually present in social settings for years, well into adulthood.

# Telepathic Tendencies?

Twins frequently told of a "special language," whether it was toddlers communicating effectively to each other in language indecipherable to parent eavesdroppers, adolescent twins who made up their own language to the exclusion of other peers, or the unintelligible "dialogues" twins have with each other in their sleep. And sometimes words aren't necessary at all—there is just a deep, indescribable connection.

Common are the stories of "twin powers." Twin interviewee Anne, now in her forties, described an incident from her teen years. She was out shopping alone with her mother when she just intuited that something was wrong. She was a young teenager at the time, and her twin brother Sal was out with a friend. She urged her mother to return to the house because something was wrong with Sal. Her mother dismissed the concern as unreasonable, but after Anne's passionate insistence, her mother gave in and they returned to the house. When they got there, there was a message from the police on the answering machine: Sal had been in a serious car accident.

Other twins reported that as adults, one would sense that something was wrong with their twin and would feel the need to call to check in. Oftentimes, there was indeed something wrong: the twin sibling was suffering from a significant emotional or physical injury. JP reported this inexplicable sensation he started having as a teenager and still has, now as an adult in his thirties: "Sometimes, I would just be sitting around, hanging out, and I would feel goose bumps and my heart would start to race a little. And then [his twin]'s face would pop in my head, and I just knew something was wrong. I would text her, and if she didn't respond, I'd call her husband. And I was always right." JP also reported that he would sense chills and a weird euphoric feeling randomly, and that also correlated with something positive happening in his sister's life at that moment (like when she got engaged). Notably, "it only works one way." His twin sister never felt strange sensations about him.

Another twin, Polly, recalls when she was taken by her father to the department store to buy a winter coat while her sister was taken to a different store with her mother. When they reconvened at home, they discovered that they each picked out the same exact winter coat. There were many other examples in which the twins demonstrated that they shared identical interest in clothes, celebrity idols, or hobbies without prior direct influence from each other.

Identical twin children who shared a bed as children reported that they've woken up and discussed their scary dreams with each other—their *identical* scary dreams.

Identical twins Amber and Renee had many telepathic moments. Once, Renee was working at a clothing store in the neighborhood; her mother would drive her there after school and pick her up at the end of her shift. Amber and her mom were talking

There is no doubt that there is genetic similarity in dizygotic twins and even more so in monozygotic twins (but note that more recent research has concluded that monozygotic twins do not share perfectly identical DNA). Experts have thus recommended that monozygotic twins inform their health care providers of the health history of their twin siblings, in addition to that of their other family members. In fact, observing the health trajectory of one's twin sibling could help guide a twin in navigating her own health issues. Perplexingly, whether one is a twin is not an inquiry on current medical history forms.

one night, and Amber looked at the clock and saw that it was 8:53 p.m. "Renee!" she called out to her mom, "We have to pick up Renee!" They drove to the store to pick up Renee, and when she got in the car, Renee said to Amber, "You know, it's so weird. I was closing up the cash register when I thought I heard you calling my name. I looked at the clock and saw that it was 8:53 p.m., and I was like, *That's weird—it's too early for her to be here.* I went to the door to let you in, and you weren't there."

One of my favorite anecdotes was from Stephanie. She and her twin brother were told to take out the trash one cold winter morning, and neither of them wanted to. They agreed to a best-of-three match of Rock, Paper, Scissors. Stephanie laughed, "We kept doing the same thing, round after round—we both did rock or we both did scissors. It was a never-ending game. It got to the point where I just gave up and volunteered to take out the trash because I was tired of sitting there, waiting for one of us to win!"

There is a charming, well-known story of twins who were raised apart from the age of four weeks and were finally reunited at the age of thirty-nine. When Jim Lewis and Jim Springer reunited, they discovered some amazing similarities: they had both been named "James" by their adoptive families, who did not know each other; they had both had dogs named Troy; and they had both been married twice—their first wives were both named Linda and their second wives were both named Betty. They also both suffered from tension headaches, smoked the same brand of cigarettes, drove the same car, and vacationed at the same beach in Florida.

There's another story of twin girls who were separated before turning a year old and raised in separate homes. As young adults who had never come in contact with another, they each were nail-biters, hypochondriacs, afraid of the dark, and fearful of being left alone. There are countless stories of twins who were separated at birth yet ended up securing the same job title in the same industry, enjoying the same favorite foods, joining the same religious sect and political party, and even marrying individuals with the same name.

Some scientists will debunk the theory that these similarities occurring in twins demonstrate telepathic tendencies, and they will describe the seemingly uncanny phenomena in less supernatural terms. They opine that rather than an actual psychic connection, the twins are simply the product of similar thinking patterns and being raised in the same environment, and, as some might posit, they are experiencing pure coincidence. These experts note that there are finite pools of significant characteristics in our lives. There are only so many brands of cigarettes and a limited number of different foods on the market. And all of these chattels which twins might choose in common could also lead to other similarities that they manifest: for instance, lung cancer or obesity.

American male twins in their forties are more likely to marry a woman named Jennifer than a woman with any other name. But the apparent coincidence is not as remarkable as we might think. Indeed, American male non-twins are just as likely to marry a Jennifer. Also, there are an estimated one hundred million sets of twins worldwide. Based on the documented stories of these mysterious twin connections, it would appear that more than 99 percent of sets of twins have not experienced these notable connections. So if your twins do not have telepathic tendencies, they are in good company!

## The Secret Club

Regardless of zygosity, twins who are raised together typically have a strong bond with one another that eclipses all other relationships. One twin interviewee said, "if the twin bond is successful, there is nothing more powerful." Another twin interviewee described the charm of the relationship as feeling like she "belonged to a secret club that not everyone is a member of." Most twins felt fortunate to be a twin and used words like "cool," "fun," and "neat" to describe the experience. When asked if they might have preferred not living every moment of one's life with a twin, most twins responded that they couldn't possibly imagine living life without a twin. They didn't know any different and had trouble even fantasizing about growing up as a singleton. One twin said that she doesn't like to think about growing old because that leads to thoughts of her twin sister dying and that thought is "too much to bear."

Studies show that for identical twins who were separated at birth and then reunited later, about 80 percent reported feeling emotionally closer to their newly discovered sibling than they did to their best friends. Researchers conclude from this data that there's a strong genetic component in the bond between identical twins.

Twins Malcolm and Tanesha have been very close their entire lives. Malcolm was always in the advanced placement tracks in middle and high schools, while Tanesha was in the less-gifted academic track. Malcolm became a professional in academia, while Tanesha tried to succeed as a musician and eventually ended up in sales. And despite the fact that they ran in different social groups and had generally different interests, they still label their past relationship "very close." As adults now in their mid-fifties reflecting on their friendship, they acknowledge how different they have always been. They are still each other's "best friend in the whole world," yet Malcolm noted that "if we weren't twins, I'm not sure we'd even be friends."

For my daughters, in infancy, they didn't seem to recognize that there was another baby competing for attention and sharing in the limited resources until they could turn their heads and look at each other. Before that, they were physically next to each other most of the time but didn't seem to register the presence of the other, despite hearing the other's cries.

Some of the twins I interviewed, however, were drawn to each other even as very young newborns. These twins were told by their parents that, as newborns, they would reach for one another when separated. Another set were told that their mother would try to keep them physically separate in one bassinet and one would inevitably roll into the other so they could cuddle with each other.

Even though my twin daughters didn't seem to have that special bond as newborns, as they grew into young children, they seemed to show more fondness for each other. When they were toddlers just learning to speak, Eden opened a magazine to an advertisement that showed two kittens spooning each other during a nap. "Eden and Tal," she said, smiling, as she moved her finger up and down on the page, pointing to the two kittens. (As if the image of two kittens cuddling in a photo wasn't cute enough, now my toddler daughter was comparing herself and her sister with the kittens—Gah! A mom's heart can only take so much swelling!)

Many twins commented that having a twin meant having a keen self-awareness. A twin is one's "mirror." One twin interviewee enjoyed witnessing her twin sibling interacting with other people in order to understand how she interacts with other people and how people react to her.

Living arrangements also often served to intensify the twin bond. For all the same-sex twins who shared a room until they left their house for college, approximately half shared a room due to their preference for doing so, while half were forced together due to lack of alternate bedroom availability. None of the male/female twins I interviewed shared a bedroom beyond the elementary school years. For the twins who had separate bedrooms, many would hang out in one of their bedrooms to do homework together and then return to their separate spaces to sleep. Many times, they would have weeknight "sleepovers" in one of their rooms because they were chatting late at night in the same bed and inadvertently fell asleep that way.

Not surprisingly, twins who grew up to parent their own children often reported that in filling out guardianship paperwork, their twin sibling was the immediate and obvious choice for the guardian of their children in the event of an untimely death. For many twins, the relationship is a close one. And it is unlike any other relationship with friends or other family members.

## The Twin Bond and Death

In a 2016 *Guardian* article about the remarkable bond that twins share, nine-year-old twin Xanthe poignantly stated, "[My twin] Yazmyne always says to me, 'How sad would you be if I died?' And I always say, 'I would be so sad that I would die, too.'"[2]

There is an area of research measuring the loss and grief suffered by twins when their twin siblings die. Monozygotic twins tend to suffer more greatly than dizygotic twins, but both sets generally feel a greater sense of grief than their non-twin counterparts do when they lose a sibling or close family member. Twins also suffer more acutely when their co-twins die than when they experience the loss of any other relative or friend, with the exception of a partner or spouse.

Twins who lose one another have the burden that others undergo with a significant loss: the redefining of oneself. Like a woman who has lost her husband of fifty years, a twin must also figure out how to define herself in the absence of her twin. *Am I still a twin?* It could be argued that twins might have it harder than the bereaved spouse: whereas the spouse can recall a time when she was not "John's wife," the twin has only ever known what it is like to be a twin with a living twin sibling.

Jerome and his twin sister Emily were in their thirties when Emily died. They were close as children and relatively close with each other as adults, as reported to me by Jerome's wife. Now, almost ten years since her death, Jerome still cannot comfortably discuss the circumstances of Emily's death or his feelings about it. His and Emily's birthday as well as the anniversary of her death are particularly difficult days for him. There was a special antique chair that Jerome acquired from her house after her passing that had remained hidden in his basement. Jerome's wife told me that recently, Jerome finally agreed to display the chair in their living room. Jerome's wife believes this might be a sign that he is starting to heal from the grief he has been suffering since Emily's death.

Identical twins Cody and Teddi were best friends throughout childhood and young adulthood. For their entire lives, they spoke to each other at least once or twice a day. "We always spoke to each other right before bed, too, if for no other reason than to say goodnight to each other. Sometimes that call would be at three in the morning, but it was always just understood that she would be the last person I spoke to before going to sleep." When they were in their twenties, Teddi was tragically killed in a car accident. Upon learning of her sister's death, Cody reported that her first thought was *How am I supposed to live without her?* Cody was in grief-stricken disbelief because she couldn't conceptualize how she could "go every day without hearing Teddi's voice." It took years for Cody to find comfort and peace. Cody attributes her healing to realizing that she could replace talking *to* Teddi every day with talking *about* her and keeping her memory alive.

Where the cause of death of a twin is a heritable disease, the surviving co-twin tends to reframe his expectations of mortality. Interviewees told me that they may even take certain precautions to ward off their perceived inevitable concession to disease: change their diet, improve other lifestyle habits, and undergo more frequent health checks.

## The Twin Bond Boosts Longevity

A 2016 study from the Danish Twin Registry produced an interesting conclusion about the longevity of twins. The Registry accumulated data from more than 2,900 pairs of same-sex twins born in Denmark between 1870 and 1900. They compared their mortality rates to that of the general non-twin Danish population. The study found that identical twins live longer than fraternal twins and that fraternal twins live longer than non-twins.[3]

I could just leave you with that statistic, but I feel compelled to discuss the marriage protection effect from the 1990s. Studies from that decade showed that individuals who were married enjoyed overall better health than those who were not married. The researchers theorized that people who are in close, intimate, loving relationships (which marriages are idealized to be) are healthier because they have someone who cares about them and would help protect them from illness and calamity. But the critics questioned this conclusion. They posited that we cannot conclude that marriage itself makes you healthier. Perhaps instead it's just that healthier people are more likely to get married.

Why is this relevant to the discussion of the Danish Twin Registry study? Because with the Danish twin study, there is no such concern with the conclusion about twin longevity. To wit, unlike the marriage study, we can logically conclude that twins are healthier and live longer—and we cannot say that those who are healthier and live longer are twins. In other words, while you can *choose* to marry (and thus call into question the marriage protection effect), you cannot *choose* to be a twin. Thus, when you conclude that twins live longer than non-twins because they're in close relationships, there's less doubt that it's the close relationship itself that improves longevity.

The twin study's conclusion corroborates the larger body of research that has tried to prove that close social relationships of any type are good for your health.

## The Bond Is Not Always Strong

Some twin interviewees reported that their parents would tell them, "your twin is your best friend, and he will be there for you always." Because there is so much hype built around the twin bond, it seems almost unnatural for twins to not feel very close to their twin sibling. The messaging in our society is that twins inevitably share a special bond. As a result, when twins do not feel that way about each other, they may feel abnormal, ashamed, or guilty.

It is imperative for parents of twins to try to reduce any external pressure society may be imposing on the children, making them feel that they must be close to each other and must be each other's best friend. The message needs to be that siblings, whether the same age or not, sometimes get along really well and sometimes fight—and that is all normal. If your twins are not each other's best friends, you have not failed as a parent and they have not failed as siblings. While having children who are emotionally close to each other is rewarding for a parent to witness, it is not shameful for the parent or abnormal for the child when the twins' bond is not very strong. For dizygotic twins, in particular, they are simply siblings who happen to share a womb and birth date. Imagine if we expected all siblings (regardless of birth date) to be best friends with one another!

# Tips for Celebrating (but Not Overemphasizing) the Unique Companionship

- Start discussions early in life about who your children are and the circumstances of their birth.
- Provide adequate emotional support and intervene if you witness an unhealthy emotional codependency develop between your twin children.
- Enjoy the specialness of your children's relationship and marvel at their similarities and dissimilarities from afar.
- Schedule singular playdates so each child can have a chance to bond with another non-sibling child at his own pace and without the presence of his twin sibling.
- Encourage the use of inanimate transitional objects, like lovies or soft blankets.
- Enable each child to undergo a "first" milestone alone, without the presence or parallel experience of her twin sibling.
- Don't make your children feel personally responsible for each other's happiness or sadness.
- Encourage empathy (but not a feeling of emotional dependency) between the two.
- Support your children when they want to develop close relationships outside of the twinship.
- Normalize their relationship, whatever it is. Do not create expectations of being each other's best friend—or archrival.

1. Jeffrey Kluger, *The Sibling Effect: What the Bonds among Brothers and Sisters Reveal about Us* (New York: Riverhead Books, 2011), 124.

2. Lizzie Pook, "'I've Never Needed Anyone Else': Life as an Identical Twin," *The Guardian*, October 29, 2016, https://www.theguardian.com/lifeandstyle/2016/oct/29/identical-twin-never-needed-anyone-else.

3. David J. Sharrow and James J. Anderson, "A Twin Protection Effect? Explaining Twin Survival Advantages with a Two-Process Mortality Model," *PLoS ONE* 11, no. 5 (2016): e0154774, http://journals.plos.org/plosone/article/file?id=10.1371/journal.pone.0154774&type=printable.

## CHAPTER TWO

# Encourage Individuality

*I am not a phenomenon; I'm a person.*

—David

I n the episode "Dr. Hell No" of the humorous sitcom *Black-ish*, Pops (played by Laurence Fishburne) is roughhousing with one of his grandchildren, who is a twin. "Be careful!" yells Pops's son Dre (Anthony Anderson). "He's half of a set!" While it makes for good television to refer to twins humorously that way, in reality, parents should be highlighting the uniqueness of each child.

My own daughters, in whom I try so hard to instill a sense of individuality and uniqueness, still sometimes frame their own identities within the twinship. For instance, at the three-year old wellness visit at the pediatrician, any time she asked Eden a question, Eden would respond for herself and then for her sister Tal, who was not present. The pediatrician, like any good kid-friendly doctor, was trying to engage Eden in conversation so Eden wouldn't focus on the medical tools and instruments that were probing her.

The doctor asked, "What's your favorite color?"

Eden replied, "My favorite color is pink, and Tal's favorite color is blue."

"What do you like to eat for dinner?"

Eden answered, "I like toast, and Tal likes pizza."

This pattern of pointed questions and gratuitous responding continued for the whole appointment. The doctor never once asked about Tal, Tal wasn't in the room, and Tal's wellness visit wasn't for another two weeks. Yet Eden made sure Tal was, at least by name and basic information, present.

When it was finally time for Tal's appointment, she did not answer for Eden at all. All of Tal's answers were directly responsive to the question, and Eden's name was not mentioned once. When we returned to school after the appointment, however, Tal made sure to tell her classmates that she didn't cry when the doctor gave her a shot but that Eden had cried when she was given a shot at the doctor. It was true; Eden had cried. And Eden was always the first to share that fact with anyone who asked. But at the time Tal was sharing that information, nobody had asked about Eden. Still, Tal saw fit to compare (and distinguish) her disposition at the doctor's office from that of Eden. So even with my best attempts to help them have unique and individualized moments, my daughters often found a way to turn these singular moments into joint experiences.

I spent a lot of time interviewing identical twins Fred and Lawrence, who were very forthcoming. While interviewing Fred,

I noticed he seemed to reflect on his childhood with rose-colored glasses. He didn't mind that his mother dressed him and Lawrence alike. He loved sharing his birthday party with Lawrence. He was tickled when people confused him with Lawrence. And then I interviewed Lawrence. One of the first things he said was, "Fred spent many years trying to prove how alike we were. And I spent many years trying to prove how different we were." He later said, "Fred fiercely loved being a twin, and I fiercely wanted to be independent."

In a 2016 *Guardian* article on identical twins, the statements of nine-year-old twins Yazmyne and Xanthe were notably similar:

*Yazmyne:* I hate spending time apart. I love wearing the same clothes and always encourage Xanthe to do it, but she never lets me. Sometimes I get very sad when people say we are starting to look different. I like being a twin and looking the same. I always want it to be that way.

*Xanthe:* I like it, too, but sometimes I think it would make a good change to be split up occasionally. Because we will have to do that some day, and it might help us.[1]

And yet, when asked whether one would have preferred not being a twin, many twins remarked that they had no idea because they simply could not imagine it. As one interviewee reported, "People ask me what it's like to be a twin, and I say, 'Compared to what?'" For us singletons, it's fascinating to think of how life would be with a twin but impossible to truly comprehend.

Still, without a true understanding, try your best to imagine experiencing almost every moment in life with another person who is the same age, has the same number of siblings and parents, has the same last name, lives in your house, goes to the same school, has the same teacher, has the same toys, and goes through life on the same waking, eating, playing, napping, bathing, and sleeping schedule as you. That is how many twins go through their early years of life.

From the moment my twin daughters Eden and Tal could speak, they indicated that they thought they were interchangeable—at least in nomenclature. When Eden would point to a photo of Tal, she would say "Eden," and vice versa. When we would ask her to point to Tal, she would point to herself or to her sister, at varying times. Tal did the same, referring to herself or her photographic image as "Tal" or "Eden" interchangeably. (I should remind the reader that my twins are fraternal and look nothing alike!)

Linguistic studies of twins confirm the universality of this language tendency displayed by my daughters. Researchers found that in the first years of speech, twins often use a double name to refer to themselves as a unit ("Tal-Eden" or "Eden-Tal"). They also tend to use singular verbs in reference to themselves together ("Tal-Eden takes a bath") and a singular pronoun to describe themselves together (e.g., "Which one of me is this?" while pointing to a photo of both twins).

The individuation process for young children is usually assisted by a close relationship with the primary caregiving parent. Quality time with the primary caregiving parent will give children the exclusive emotional support and feeling of security that they need to feel confident to seek autonomy. Yet a parent of twins has much more interrupted interaction with each child and less time and opportunity to devote exclusive emotional support, resulting in a delayed process for individuation for the child.

Identity, independence, and individuality are essential to a person's emotional health. Studies have shown that twins have more difficulty than non-twins in developing these attributes. A child's sense of self and individuation is formed very early. For twins, the process is complicated by the necessity to not only separate from the parent but also separate from the twin sibling. The task is confounded even further for identical twins, who are often mistaken for one another by friends and even family. Twins at this age thus may not take appropriate steps to try to individuate from each other.

The formation of one's sense of personhood and identity is boosted again in adolescence when an individual tries to separate further from parents, home, and upbringing. They are questioning the values and ideals with which they were raised and trying to figure out which of those they will keep or discard. They may find comfort in aligning with a peer group or clique. In *Things Will Be Different for My Daughter: A Practical Guide to Building Her Self-Esteem and Self-Reliance*, authors Mindy Bingham and Sandy Stryker note that in adolescence, this peer group identity overcomes individual identity and that "[t]here is safety and security in the group identity as they move from who their parents want them to be and struggle to find out who they are."[2] This essential process is complicated in twins who, generally, have trouble discovering their unitary identity because they view themselves as part of a pair. Even if they, as a set, have separated from their parents, they still have not formed their unitary identity because they have not separated from each other.

And after they learn how to separate from each other, they have to prove their differences to everyone else. Twins, unlike singletons, are brought into the world with a peer against whom the world will compare them from day one. They have to face the presumption of others that they are the same person. Twins thus carry an extra burden of proof that their singleton counterparts do not.

In her book *The Sister Knot: Why We Fight, Why We're Jealous, and Why We'll Love Each Other No Matter What*, Dr. Terri Apter explains that siblings typically strive to distinguish themselves from one another so that they can gain new attention from their parents. It's easier, after all, to win the competition for parental love when you are competing only against yourself. Thus, when children grow up together in the same family, they feel the need to be viewed as distinct and separate from the other children. The drive to be different from one's sibling is seemingly even greater for twins who may share more genetic similarities than singleton siblings. Dr. Apter highlights the fact that identical twins who were raised apart are more likely to be similar to each other than those who were raised in the same household. "Growing up together," she notes, "identifying with one another, is a good way to ensure differences."[3]

Kim was thankful when her parents allowed her and her identical sister to go to different high schools. This, she reported, helped them thrive socially and academically, compared to when they were in the same school. But even though she made sincere attempts to develop her own identity, she still found herself using language that suggested that she was one part of a whole. "Sometimes I'd be talking to someone who didn't know I was a twin, and I was describing something from childhood and I'd say, 'And then we went to the store where we saw this and that and we were worried about . . .' Whatever. And the person would look at me like I was crazy. But that's just how I saw my childhood—she was always there, so all my stories are 'we' stories."

Lance also struggled to find his own identity outside of his twinship with his brother Phil, with whom he was very close. In social settings, if Lance was loud, Phil would be quiet. If Phil was hyper, Lance would be calm. They just knew how to "be" when they were together. But when Phil started to date his partner seriously, Lance felt "out of sorts." He explained, "I was so used to being with Phil socially that I didn't know how that worked without him. I couldn't quite find my place if it wasn't by his side, working off of him. It's funny because I had always wanted people to treat us as individuals, but when the time came to be an individual, I didn't really know what to do; I didn't know who I was—like who I was supposed to be—as an individual."

Some twins reported to me that they did not follow their own preferences just so they could be perceived as different from their twin siblings. Allison and Kate were identical twins who, as children, looked very similar to one another and whom family and friends would constantly confuse for one another. In their rural town, there were not a lot of opportunities for extracurricular activities, and when Allison chose to take a gymnastics class, Kate, who was also interested in gymnastics, chose instead to take swimming lessons just to distinguish herself from Allison. As an adult, Kate wonders whether she would have excelled in gymnastics. Eventually, not following one's own inclinations will yield frustration, confusion, and increased identity issues. Twins need to be true to themselves and find ways to establish their identities in spite of the presence of a same-age sibling who may or may not share the same interests. Encouraging individuality between one's twin children is thus, arguably, the most imperative of all parenting endeavors and, notably, not the most difficult.

Another impediment to a twin child's sense of individuality is the constant message that she must share with her twin sibling. Constant forced sharing interferes with a child's sense of self; it disenables a child from realizing that she is entitled to enjoy an item alone, in her own time, and on her own terms. She loses a sense of entitlement to be herself and enjoy her own things in the world.

When twins do establish their own respective senses of individuality, their identity formation is still different from their non-twin counterparts because they have the added identity marker of being a twin. Yes, they are individuals, but they are also integral members of a team they did not choose to join.

At any age, a trap into which many twins fall is allowing their twin siblings to problem-solve for them. A twin will often allow (or even request) his twin sibling to resolve his conflicts. This prevents the requestor from developing his own problem-solving skills and burdens the requested with an obligation that is otherwise not his responsibility. Ultimately, both children have been denied an opportunity for individualized personal growth.

Parents can also inadvertently discourage individuation. In a study about mothers' child-rearing attitudes toward their children, researchers found that mothers of identical twins had a greater tendency than mothers of fraternal twins to dress their children alike and raise them in parallel or symmetrical environments. It can be hard for a parent to resist the positive attention she receives from the outside world when others are quick to marvel at the delight of two same-age siblings. When having twins is so celebrated, there is pressure on twin children to play to the expected stereotypes of twins and further the fantasy. Parents of monozygotic twins tended to treat their children as two halves of a whole, more so than parents of dizygotic twins. Research further suggests that twins who were treated as a solitary unit by their parents had more difficulty forming their individual identities than twins who were treated more distinctly.

Regardless, so ingrained is a twin's sense of twinship from an early age that most twins will not discover that they are unique in their twinship until preschool years. Before then, they tend to assume that everyone has a twin sibling. During preschool, they discover that most children do not have a twin sibling and that they are different in that respect.

In Chapter One, I described how twins tend to use one another as a transitional object. When a child has another individual who can soothe him, it is a great boon to parents who are otherwise unavailable, but it may impede a twin's ability to self-soothe and develop emotional independence. Bingham and Stryker write, "Self-esteem depends on the development of a healthy sense of self, a person's own understanding, and acceptance of who she really is."[4] Trouble forming one's identity can thus be linked to low self-esteem, codependence, and difficulty developing healthy relationships outside of the twin relationship. However, while these undesirable consequences can, in extreme cases, result in the children failing to form a healthy identity, most twins do not fall into this category. Most twins are simply delayed in the process as opposed to completely failing to undergo the process.

The subject of this chapter—encouraging individuality—is a piece of advice I was given by every single adult twin I interviewed. In fact, it was the only piece of advice delivered by adult twins and triplets that was universal for everyone. I gleaned from my interviews that twins felt a deeper sense of urgency in establishing their own identities than non-twins. In the rest of this chapter, I'll discuss some of the main areas in which twins need or seek individuality.

## Personalities

Bingham and Stryker note the importance of people carving their own paths. For girls and women, the imperative is even greater. "If they are unable to find recognition in the larger world, girls and women tend to seek acceptance on a smaller scale by becoming determined 'people pleasers,' by looking for recognition from others that they are worthwhile human beings."[5] Professor Sally Archer opines that girls and women are socialized to be what they perceive others want them to be. I would argue that twins (of any gender) face this same risk; by not having a sense of unique individuality, they might navigate the world with a constant need to seek assurances and acceptance from the people around them.

Apter describes the importance of being perceived as unique by others. She emphasizes that the need to see oneself as unique runs even deeper. "Being ourselves," she writes, "and somehow taking ownership of ourselves, has vastly different meanings to different people; but self-recognition has become as necessary as air."[6]

Many interviewees observed that their parents, relatives, and friends often incorrectly assumed that the twins shared the same personality traits, same fears, and same senses of humor.

Twins Tamekah and Shawn spent practically every day of their childhood lives together. Tamekah had trouble recalling one instance in her childhood where she and Shawn were separated from each other for anything more than the occasional doctor's appointment. She reported:

> I felt frustrated that every conversation I had with my parents was with me and Shawn. They always spoke to us as a group, never individually. Shawn, who had a stronger personality, ended up speaking first and ultimately deciding for both of us, even when I didn't always agree. He seemed to always talk on my behalf, and I guess I let him; I would always just go along with everything. Now that I'm older and not always with Shawn, I've learned to speak up for myself. But I think if my parents had talked to me privately, they would have learned more about me and what I really wanted—and maybe I would have developed more confidence earlier on in life.

Twin interviewees advised that parents should take the time to learn who their children are as individuals—what makes each child tick? What causes each child to be anxious? What pleases and displeases each child? In what areas is the child confident? In what areas does the child lack self-esteem? Learn the differences and nuances, and show the child that you understand him for who he is—as a separate entity from his twin sibling.

Parents often lament when their child is obsessed with a sport, a television character, or a song. Here's an example from my household: Like many other households during the same time period, Disney's *Frozen* empire consumed our home. We owned a digital version of the movie, we had the soundtrack on our iPhones, and we owned every tchotchke known to man in the likeness of Elsa, Anna, or Olaf. Indeed, from decorative hair accessories to nightlights, we were constantly reminded that *Frozen* was an inextricable part of our quotidian living.

If there was one word to describe my demeanor during this time, it would be *grinch*. I was so annoyed at all the consumerism. *Yes, it is a good movie. Yes, the characters are charming. Yes, the songs have catchy lyrics and melodies. But, come on! Olaf-shaped pasta?! Did it need to come to this?*

But as I delved more deeply into my research of the emotional health of twins, I stopped bemoaning the *Frozen* hype. I considered that I had been raising my daughters in more or less the same world. They attended the same school, slept and woke on the same schedule, and ate at the same time each day. At the end of school, my question—"How was your day?"—was lodged at both of them at the same time. But they had different days and different answers. There were so many missed opportunities throughout the day—opportunities when I could have asked one child one question, where I could have explored each child's respective uniqueness. But how and when could I do this?

The answer: when I'm discussing *Frozen*. Each child surely likes different things about the movie. Each child might have her own favorite character, song, or scene. This is my chance to really get to know each child individually. Find out what makes her tick. Find out what she likes and explore the reasons behind it. How do you get your young child to talk? Bring up a Disney movie and ask specific questions.

So when I hear *Frozen*'s "Let It Go" for the millionth time, my first instinct is along the lines of scratching my ears off my head. But then I remind myself that my child's deep interest in this phenomenon presents a wonderful opportunity for me to bond with her.

This attempt to get to know one's child individually is so important for parents of twins who rarely give their twins regular, individualized attention. This is the chance to get to know the idiosyncrasies of each child and to make each child feel special and unique. Parents of twins have the bonus of making each child feel unique and distinct from her twin sibling because, inevitably, what drives her to like something will be different from what drives her twin to like something—even if that "something" is the same thing! So I urge parents to make each child feel special by showing interest in that which interests the child. Every child deserves to feel understood and cherished for who she, alone, is.

## Talents

Imagine a non-twin child who has an ear for language. He grasps the writing and pronunciation in his French class at a level well beyond that of his peers. He sounds like a natural-born French citizen when he conversationally discusses the weather. Now imagine that the little Francophile has a sister five years his junior. Would the parent of these children expect the little sister to share the same interest and proclivity in the French language? Probably not. Yet many parents of twin siblings make an assumption that specific talents are shared. This can pave the way for an unfair and unhealthy comparison (see Chapter Six).

The adult twins I interviewed wished their parents hadn't compared them as they participated in sports, music, academics, and the arts. Some twins appreciated that parents allowed them to play different musical instruments and participate in different extracurricular activities, even though it was more of a difficult logistical endeavor for the parent, shuttling each child to his respective lesson, tournament, or concert. As adults, these twin interviewees understood how difficult it was for their parents to ensure that each child arrived to, and was picked up from, his respective activity on time. And, as adults, they reflected on how beneficial it was for them to have a chance to shine in their own rights without the looming shadow of their twin siblings. It was a relief for them to have at least one activity in which they didn't have to compete with their twin. They also enjoyed the socialization and ability to form bonds with friends that were different from their twin's friends.

It can seem like a logistical nightmare to shuttle each child to a different location with the correct equipment on the same day. Parents of twins have to be more creative than parents of singletons. Carpooling certainly helps in these cases! Again, when your kids are older and well adjusted, they will thank you. Until then, bite your tongue, grit your teeth, get the thankless job done, and hope that at least on Mother's Day or Father's Day, you get a nice photo mug for your office.

## Social Circles

Twin children don't need to have the same friends. Of course, there are friends whom they might share and genuinely like, notwithstanding their connection to each other, but to help develop healthy non-sibling friendships, it is imperative for a parent to schedule separate playdates.

It is more convenient for a parent to schedule one playdate for both children. It requires much less time, travel, and logistical coordination than if the parent has to schedule separate playdates for each child. A parent of toddler-age twins will find it simply impossible to schedule separate playdates as she cannot leave a very young toddler alone at friend's house and obviously cannot be in two places at once. Still, as the twin children age and their independence develops, it is essential to figure out the logistics and send your twin children to separate places to develop social relationships with different peers.

Many of the adult twins I interviewed resented always having their twin sibling along for every social engagement. This hindered their ability to develop individualized and close friendships. Through adolescence and the teenage years, many twins felt obligated to "bring my sister/brother along" to social outings even where the accompanying twin was not really "part of that crowd."

Parents of non-twin children who have regular playdates with twin children have told me that their children often have a clear preference for one twin over the other yet don't know how to request a one-on-one playdate without running the risk of offending the parent or one of the twin children. A parent of twins, however, should be open to that dialogue; in fact, a parent of twins might want to open up the conversation himself.

Let's pretend that your twin children are friendly with a boy named Dylan. You could say to Dylan's parent something like, "I understand that Dylan might develop a preference for one of my children, and that's totally okay. In fact, that's natural and I would expect it to happen. I want you to feel comfortable coming to me with that information or any discussion about our children's relationships. I am more than happy to set up playdates that involve Dylan and his preferred playmate, and I will do my best to make the other child not feel left out. And with some planning, I can make sure that the other child has a playdate with someone else scheduled for the same time. Again, please feel comfortable discussing this with me at any point during their friendship with Dylan."

Social etiquette can be hard for any parent to navigate. And parents of twins have a unique circumstance that may require a little extra assertiveness and thoughtfulness.

# Appearance

Having twin babies means that, despite requests to the contrary, a parent will receive gifts of matching onesies, blankets, and other layette items. You may choose to dress your children in these matching clothes regularly, but doing so will make the distinction between them more challenging, especially in the newborn phase when there are generally fewer physical characteristics with which to distinguish them. (When my daughters were born, they had no hair and their tiny features looked so similar to me. It's amazing because beyond infancy, they look nothing alike; you wouldn't even think they were related!) Parents can do themselves a favor by dressing their babies differently, at the very least until they establish a quick visual cue as to which child is which.

Aside from ease of administration of care, you might wish to dress your twin babies differently so that you can begin to train yourself and others to think of the babies as unique individuals. Dressing your twins differently is a tool to use all through their infancy and early childhood.

Remi's parents dressed her and her identical sister alike all through their childhood. Not only were they always dressed in matching shirts, skirts, socks, and shoes, but Remi's mother even made sure that their hair bands were the same color. Remi says that she looks at childhood photos now and has no idea which one she is and which one is her sister. This did not seem to bother

Remi ("I think it's hilarious"), although more twins than not reported disliking having been forced to wear matching outfits.

If you feel comfortable, as an expecting parent you may wish to add a note to your baby registry suggesting non-matching gifts ("*We would love distinct outfits, rather than matching outfits, for these two unique bundles of pure joy! Thanks.*"). Some of us might have mothers or fathers who would be horrified if we added that note to our registry, so if gently guiding your gift-giving friends and family is not a viable option, you can still easily manage the matching items you do receive. For instance, you can accept two of the same shirt and simply not dress your babies in them at the same time.

Some givers of the matching clothes may be tickled to see a photo of the children in the matching outfits, but there's no rule in the etiquette book that says children have to be wearing the matching outfits at the same time or in the same picture. You can take two photos: one of one child wearing the outfit and another photo of the other child wearing the outfit. Sending these two photos to the giver will show an appreciation for both items while also sending the discrete but important message that your two children are unique individuals and not—as Dre from *Black-ish* would say—two halves of a set.

In toddlerhood, children may wish to start dressing themselves. Parents could set out a couple of choices of possible outfits, and some twins may choose to match each other while some may not. Parents may be surprised to see the results of their children's newfound freedom. Whether the children decided to dress similarly or differently, the exercise might give insight into how they see themselves vis-à-vis their twin sibling.

Derek and his twin brother are African-American fraternal twins whose parents dressed them alike as babies and toddlers. When they were in elementary school, they were permitted to pick out their own clothes. Derek reported, "We ended up still dressing alike. I was dark-skinned and he had light skin, so there was no risk of confusion. We just thought it was cool to go out in the same shirts, like we were part of the same sports team."

Triplet Alecia tells a fun story about choosing her own wardrobe. All through childhood, Alecia's mother bought her and her sisters matching outfits; they dressed the same until they were in middle school, when they requested the opportunity to shop for their own clothes. The mother drove them to a popular clothing store, and this is what happened:

> My mother released us at the front of the store to go explore on our own, and we all ran excitedly in different directions. We ended up in the dressing rooms around the same time, and when we emerged to look at our new outfits, we saw that we were all wearing the same thing!

It took more attempts in different stores, but soon the triplets were able to dress distinctly from one another.

What's important to learn from Derek's and Alecia's stories is that they were given the permission to choose their own clothes and represent themselves to the world as they saw fit.

But as adults, many identical twins find that even dressing distinctly does not ward off confusion among others as to which twin is which.

Identical twins Christopher and Clay worked in the same high-rise building for their summer jobs after high school. One day, Clay's colleague asked him if he was okay. He affirmed that he was and asked why she thought otherwise. She said that she saw him in the elevator earlier that day and he seemed really unhappy; he didn't even acknowledge her when she wished him a good morning. "I felt awful," Clay reported. "She had seen Christopher, who doesn't know her and must have ignored her greeting. She thought it was me in the elevator and that I was just being rude. I'm so glad she said something to me so I could do damage control!" Clay then made a point to tell everyone he worked with that his identical twin brother worked in the building too, and if they saw someone who looked like Clay, there was a chance it was, in fact, Christopher. "I told them not to be upset if it looked like I was snubbing them; I wasn't," he laughed. "Chris was."

Identical twins Robert and William had a similar experience. Robert attended a university in California specializing in computer software, while William was studying urban design at a university in Oregon. William participated in a semester-long internship program with a California-based company. When he was visiting his company's headquarters in California, he was in line at a coffee shop with a colleague and made a disparaging comment about the computer tech industry. A stranger standing in front of him turned around and said, "Rob . . .?" The stranger was a work colleague of his brother, Robert, and was initially confused (and offended!) by William's snide remark.

Identical twins who experience such awkward episodes of mistaken identity often try to find ways to distinguish themselves from each other. Identical twins Brittany and Pamela looked very similar through childhood and adulthood. In their twenties, they lived in the same neighborhood. They had different social groups, as Brittany worked full time and Pamela was a stay-at-home mother. Sometimes, when Brittany would go out, perfect strangers would smile at her and say hello. "I was jarred by how friendly strangers were to me until I realized they thought I was Pamela." That was when Brittany decided to cut her hair very short. With a pixie cut, Brittany was easily distinguishable from Pamela, who had long, straight hair. Apparently, no one confused them after that drastic hairstyle change. Now in their forties, Brittany and

Pamela still coordinate their hairstyles to ensure that they will never again share the same appearance.

# Labeling

It is natural for humans to create groups and identify individuals as being part of a group. We are born with a strong drive to categorize everything. It's part of our evolutionary nature. The mental concept that "all wooly mammoths are dangerous" helped us run when we saw one. Imagine, instead, pausing and wondering about the unique characteristics of a particular mammoth and whether he would make a fine domestic companion!

Thousands of psychological studies have confirmed that humans in today's modern times continue to group and categorize. It's our way of managing and simplifying the complex world in which we live. Within social psychology is a concept that humans tend to be "cognitive misers." Just as a stingy person doesn't want to spend one penny of his wealth, so too do most humans refrain from spending one ounce of mental energy beyond what is absolutely necessary. (The fancy psychologists would say cognitive misers are those "who in the midst of a

There was a commonality of "annoying questions people ask us" among the twins I interviewed. Here is a brief list:

- "Can you read each other's minds?"
- "What's it like to be a twin?"
- "Are you each other's best friend?"
- "Is it hard to have to always share the spotlight with each other?"
- "Who's the dominant one (or 'the alpha twin')?"
- "Do you love/hate being a twin?"

complex social world engage in heuristic, unsystematic process-ing to conserve cognitive resources,"[7] but, as a cognitive miser myself, I offer you the former, less complicated definition).

Being the cognitive misers that we are, we enjoy the automatic simplification that twins present us. They are from the same fam-ily, they have the same last name, and they even have the same birthday! Categorization complete. *These two individuals shall be henceforth known in my mind as "the twins."*

As you might think, very few twin interviewees enjoyed being lumped together as "the twins." They generally hated being referred to as "the twinnies" or "the Miller twins," for instance. (I will note an exception to that generality: one particular inter-viewee went to a large high school where, among hundreds of students in his class, he appreciated being one of only four sets of twins in the entire high school. Being referred to as "one of the James twins" helped give him some stardom in a vast, loud, crowded space where one could otherwise have been easily ignored.)

When I was growing up, my brother (who, as an adult, admits that he wasn't the kindest of siblings) would call my sister and me "Lara," a combination of my name ("Dara") and my sister's name ("Lori"). I didn't mind (it was a relatively minor slight compared to other things he did to torment us!), but I could imagine how irritating this would be if I were a twin and had to constantly bat-tle inferences that I was synonymous with my co-twin. Indeed, twin interviewees complained to me that friends and family would use their names interchangeably, attach their names as one ("BradAnna"), or come up with some other joint reference ("Branna"). These individuals noted sourly that the combination of their names or joint references highlighted others' inordinate fascination with their twinships.

Triplet Dwayne complained about the worst part about being a triplet: "When people learn I'm a triplet, it's like that's the most important thing about me. They then ask a million questions about what it's like, whether we fight, if I prefer one over the other. It's like there are so many other things I want them to want to know about me, but once they learn I'm a triplet, that's all they want to talk about."

As David, a twin interviewee, put it, "I am not a phenomenon; I'm a person."

The joint labeling seemed to be even more difficult for identical twins because they were already struggling with being confused for each other. The labeling demonstrated that others either had no idea (or were not concerned with) which one was which. The labeling thus diminished their respective senses of self-worth because each person's unique characteristics were completely ignored. The joint labeling reinforced the feeling that the twins' values were summed up in the pair and that each twin was not a separate individual who had value in her own right.

# Life Experiences

*Grit. Resilience.* You've probably heard these buzzwords in recent years as the current culture of helicopter parenting has come under scrutiny. For parents of toddlers or younger children, helicopter parenting is the default—a parent must hover over his children for the first couple years of their lives. It's a parent's job to make sure his babies' and toddlers' physical and emotional needs are met and to keep them from injuring themselves (or each other!). But parents of older children may give them more space—to run at a playground, to socialize, to have conflicts with friends, etc.

If parents don't give their growing children necessary space, they will have failed to enable their children to develop an important trait in times of trouble: grit. In *Grit to Great: How Perseverance, Passion, and Pluck Take You from Ordinary to Extraordinary*, authors Linda Kaplan Thaler and Robin Koval examine how being a hard worker (not simply gifted) more often leads to great success later in life.[8] How someone bounces back after a huge setback is the barometer for how much potential she has. So it's important that we parents land the helicopters and sit back while our kids run and play and fight and make up and trip and skin knees and keep running. Not only do we need to let our kids fall, but we also need to let them get back up on their own.

But parents of twins have an extra challenge. Even when they sit back, there is someone else there trying to keep their child from falling and failing: their twin. Twin interviewees reported to me that they often did whatever they could to protect their twin: intervening in a schoolyard fight, helping their twin cheat on a test, encouraging "the popular crowd" to include their twin in an excursion, etc. And while these all sound like lovely displays of sibling loyalty, they prevent an opportunity for mental and emotional growth.

When twin children are constantly together, experiencing life with each other, each child is not able to develop his own strength and independence. Being in what one twin interviewee described as the "eternal comfort zone" as a child hinders one's ability to learn to face difficult times. Thus, twin children need to have experiences that they go through alone so that they can learn how to navigate the world on their own terms. This will better prepare them for life as adults.

Some parents may fear that by encouraging each child to develop a healthy sense of autonomy, they are inadvertently driving a wedge between the children. Parents may feel concerned that their effort to promote individual growth might backfire and create siblings who dislike each other or fail to get along. In fact, research has shown the opposite to be true. While seemingly counterintuitive, it's the twins with the well-developed senses of self who have the closest bonds. When their unique tastes, interests, and personalities are encouraged and established, they are more likely to be compatible in part because there is reduced rivalry and competition.

# Possessions

Humans of any age find great import in property. It's something we buy, sell, loan, borrow, inherit, donate, and steal. It is one of the most controversial objects in a decedent's estate or in a divorce decree. Establishing one's property line, damaging another's personal property, and managing one's intangible property (like mutual funds or stock) are subjects in countless lawsuits. What and how much we own determine socioeconomic status. Ownership of property has been shown to be closely linked to concepts of self and personal identity.

For toddlers who engage in social settings with other children, the words they learn immediately are "my" and "mine." These words are essential in their vocabulary arsenal if they want to have any sufficient amount of time to play with any particular object. Among one- and two-year-olds, there is little respect for another's space or things, and it is not long before a child will take a toy out of another child's hands without hesitation or concern for the victim. Crying, screaming, pushing, or hair-pulling ensues. While the disrespect for another's toy is natural and expected, so is the deeply felt need on the part of the victim to not have one's toy taken away. Thankfully, by age three, children generally learn to share and negotiate. Adults will marvel at the bartering behaviors between children over seemingly valueless objects, like found rocks and crumpled store receipts. And while exchange and trade skills are a sign of positive social development, underlying the milestone is the significant import of ownership of property.

In fact, the most common cause of conflict among siblings is property. Jeffrey Kluger writes, "Small children have almost no control over their world, and what little they do have concerns their possessions. They understand early on that toys that are presented to them belong to them, and while kids are perfectly willing to encroach on the property rights of another, they can't abide someone else trespassing on theirs."[9]

But simply being a better sharer should not mean that a twin child should be expected to share significantly more than a single-ton child would be. As was discussed, ownership and possession are so important in one's development of her sense of self that a twin child needs to have exclusive possession of certain objects. If she wishes not to share those objects, she should not be forced to.

For a parent of twins who is trying to help his children establish distinctive identities, it may be helpful to not simply buy two of the same toy for each child but to instead buy a distinct toy for each child. Let's say Liz gets the unicorn and Caitlyn gets the car; from the onset, it should be emphasized that "that's Liz's unicorn" and "that's Caitlyn's car." If Caitlyn is playing with the unicorn, she must surrender it to Liz the moment Liz wishes to have it back.

My friend is the mother of one child, Abigail, who is the same age as my children. When they were toddlers, we had weekly playdates with her child. Prior to playdates at my friend's house, she would say to Abigail, "Eden and Tal are coming over, and they will want to play with every toy in this playroom. If there are any toys you don't want them to play with, let's put them in this box and we'll take the box upstairs to your room." Then, during the playdate, Abigail was expected to share all of her toys that were in the playroom.

I loved this approach. It taught Abigail the importance of sharing, but it also showed her that her mother understood and respected her need to have ownership over some objects. Your twin children similarly, and arguably more so, deserve to have ownership over some things—ownership that doesn't extend beyond the child herself, not even to other family members. If you have to write the child's name or initial on the tag or the bottom of the toy, do so.

Even though they are probably more skilled at sharing than the average singleton, that does not mean your twins actually *like* sharing. As Dr. Benjamin Spock has said, "There are only two things a child will share willingly—communicable diseases and his mother's age."[10] So, while sharing is an essential skill for emotional development, you should be clear about your twins' rights to sometimes exercise sole possession.

# Birthday Parties

Twin interviewees Brennan and Gayle enjoyed sharing one birthday party every year throughout their childhood. Their mother raised them herself in a small apartment, and it was in that small apartment that she hosted the joint birthday parties. After high school, Brennan and Gayle stopped sharing birthday parties because they went to separate colleges across the country from one another. On their thirtieth birthday, Brennan's wife organized a surprise party for Brennan and Gayle. The party was hosted by Brennan and Gayle's mother in that small apartment where she had hosted all of their childhood birthday parties. "We had one sheet cake with both our names, just like old times," Brennan recalled fondly. "It was adorable. I loved it!"

However, Dr. Joan Friedman, author of *Emotionally Healthy Twins: A New Philosophy for Parenting Two Unique Children*, strongly advises that parents should host separate birthday parties for their twin children.[11] Having a separate party shows your children that you value them as individuals and gives you a chance to celebrate each child's entrance into the world. This makes perfect sense to me. Although I might hesitate for logistical or financial reasons, it does feel consistent with my other endeavors to ensure that each of my twin children understands how unique and special she is.

That being said, every single adult I interviewed had a joint birthday party with his twin or triplet siblings, and I was amazed that almost every individual expressed nothing but joy in recalling the shared occasions. The vast majority of responses were that they never resented sharing the party. When I probed a little and asked whether they would have wanted to have the celebration to themselves, they all mentioned that they were used to sharing the spotlight and did not feel less special having shared the day. To the extent that the twins had different friends, they loved the opportunity to have all the friends together in the same place at the same time.

But there was one notable exception in my interviewees: Erin. When I initially asked Erin the question about whether she and her twin brother Jason had shared birthday parties, she indicated that they had and it hadn't bothered her. She explained that sharing the day never bothered her because birthdays aren't that big of a deal to her.

Erin then recalled that, recently, she felt a little annoyed when Jason's wife called her to invite her to Jason's birthday party.

"I thought, *Uh, sure, I'll go to a party to celebrate* his *birthday, which is also* my *birthday!*" Erin was flabbergasted that her sister-in-law didn't once acknowledge that it was also Erin's birthday.

"This incident seems to have upset you," I said. "So maybe birthdays do matter to you?"

Erin paused and then said, "I don't know, maybe . . . I think birthdays never mattered to me much because I always had to share the day with someone else. Maybe I would think birthdays were more special if I was ever able to enjoy being the only birthday child."

Bert was raised in the 1940s by German immigrant parents who fostered a misogynistic culture in the house. Bert's twin sister Sabrina was treated like "a second-class citizen simply because she was a girl." Growing up, because of this unfair treatment, Sabrina was always bitter toward Bert; he was, after all, the primary beneficiary of her oppression. As adults now, Bert and Sabrina still have a strained relationship. When he calls her every six months or so (she never calls him), Sabrina sounds like she is disappointed to hear from him. Bert described her reaction this way: "Did you ever see frost come out of a phone?"

As kids, Sabrina wanted to have her own birthday party, but Bert wanted to have a shared birthday party. "My parents always did what I wanted, so we always had one birthday party. But I always wonder: if Sabrina hadn't been a twin, she would have gotten her own birthday party and that would have been something different. Maybe we would have been closer."

So while jointly celebrated birthdays can feel special because most kids don't have a same-aged companion to share the day with, some twin children might resent, rather than appreciate, the combined celebration. The problem is, it's hard to know what's best for your own twin children and, frankly, how to proceed when one of your twins prefers a shared party while the other does not.

Having separate birthday parties seems to make perfect theoretical sense and is consistent with the expert advice to foster a healthy sense of self and individuality in your twins. But perhaps a parent is wise to remain flexible on the issue rather than follow an absolute rule. Talk openly with each twin child. Have the conversation in private, with each twin individually. Ask what she prefers. If one twin prefers a separate party and the other twin does not, have two separate parties. You could explain to both children that it was your decision and desire to have separate parties for each child because you wanted to celebrate each child individually. And you don't have to break the bank: a party could be a couple of friends coming over for a sleepover or a day at the movies with some friends.

Guests will often give either one gift for both children to share or two of the same gift to each child. A twin interviewee alerted me to a small problem that I hadn't anticipated or experienced in my household. When your children receive the same gift, one child might shred the wrapping paper in mere seconds while the other child is more meticulous and careful in opening the gift. The surprise and joy of the gift-opening process is diminished for the slower twin. One strategy is to place the children in separate rooms as they unwrap their gifts; another is to place them back to back so each child can experience the joy of unwrapping the gift and discovering the bounty at her own speed.

From the various descriptions of shared birthday celebrations, I learned some helpful tricks parents can employ to make each child feel special. Parents can make or buy two cakes, each with the favorite flavor and color of each child. Alternatively, the parent can make or buy one cake with separate and distinct halves. Parents can give separate (and sometimes different) gifts. Parents can have guests sing "Happy Birthday" twice. A great example of this is Greta and Bill's mom. Greta was born two minutes before her brother Bill, so their mom would bring out Greta's cake first while singing "Happy Birthday, Greta" and, two minutes later, would bring out Bill's cake and sing "Happy Birthday, Bill."

As adults, many twins I interviewed mentioned that they always try to be physically together on their birthdays, even in cases where that would require air travel! Clearly, birthdays carry great importance for many twins, so parents should carefully consider how to approach them.

# Tips for Encouraging Individuality

- Don't choose your twins' names using rhyme (Will and Jill) or alliteration (Bessie and Bella). This reinforces the notion that they are each part of a set as opposed to two separate individuals.
- Dress your children differently. When they are old enough, encourage them to pick out their own clothes. They may choose to match each other; they may not. Allow them to decide how they wish to look and allow them to realize the consequences of their choices; this will be empowering for them.
- Don't force your children to share everything all the time. Buy them separate and distinct toys, label them accordingly, and respect their need to determine, at all times, who plays with them.
- Always refer to your children by their names rather than referring to them as "the twins." Encourage relatives and friends to do so as well.
- Relate to and converse with your children individually.
- Refer to them as individuals when talking about them, whether they can hear you or not.
- When your twin children are young, ask them questions about what they like and don't like so that you can learn early on what makes each child tick.
- Spend one-on-one time with each child (more on this in Chapter Four).

- If there are other non-twin children in the family, co-ordinate times for each twin to have separate time with the non-twin sibling(s).
- Offer or suggest different musical instruments, sports, or other activities for each child.
- If it's possible financially and logistically to put the twin children in separate rooms, do so to allow each of them to claim and decorate her own space (they can then **choose** to have sleepovers with each other!).
- If two separate rooms are not available, try to give each child a special space in the shared room (or in another room) that is his and his alone. Allow the child to decorate and organize the space as he wishes and help "protect" the space from unwanted intrusion by siblings.
- Schedule different playdates for them with different peers. Openly allow parents of your children's friends to invite one, not both, to a playdate or birthday party.
- Verbalize to your child what you observe about him; tell him about the special and unique traits he possesses.
- While sibling photos are wonderful for framing, don't forget to take individual photos of each child through-out their childhood and adulthood. (Besides, most parents find that it's much easier to encourage one child to smile for the camera at the right time rather than two!)
- Discuss having separate birthday parties with each child in private. If one child wishes to celebrate separately, honor that wish and represent the decision for separate parties as one you alone have made.
- If you are welcoming birthday gifts for your twin children, gently guide relatives and friends as to the unique and differing wish lists of each child.

- If your children are given identical gifts, separate them or have them sit back to back when opening them so they can each experience the joy and surprise of discovering the new gift.
- When celebrating their birthday, consider having two separate cakes (with each child's respective favorite flavors and decorations) and singing "Happy Birthday" twice.
- Read separate bedtime stories to them or have a partner or other caregiver read to one child on one night while you read to the other child and switch the following night.

1. Pook, "'I've Never Needed Anyone Else'."

2. Mindy Bingham and Sandy Stryker, *Things Will Be Different for My Daughter: A Practical Guide to Building Her Self-Esteem and Self-Reliance* (New York: Penguin, 1995).

3. Terri Apter, *The Sister Knot: Why We Fight, Why We're Jealous, and Why We'll Love Each Other No Matter What* (New York: W. W. Norton & Company, 2007).

4. Bingham and Stryker, *Things Will Be Different for My Daughter.*

5. Ibid.

6. Apter, *The Sister Knot.*

7. David H. Ebenbach and Dacher Keltner, "Power, Emotion, and Judgmental Accuracy in Social Conflict: Motivating the Cognitive Miser," *Basic and Applied Social Psychology* 20, no. 1 (1998): 7, http://dx.doi.org/10.1207/s15324834basp2001_2.

8. Linda Kaplan Thaler and Robin Koval, *Grit to Great: How Perseverance, Passion, and Pluck Take You from Ordinary to Extraordinary* (New York: Crown Business, 2015).

9. Kluger, *The Sibling Effect*, 41.

10. Benjamin Spock, *The Common Sense Book of Baby and Child Care* (New York: Duell, Sloan and Pearce, 1946).

11. Joan Friedman, *Emotionally Healthy Twins: A New Philosophy for Parenting Two Unique Children* (Cambridge, MA: Da Capo Press, 2008): 123–5.

# CHAPTER THREE

# Relieve the Caretaking Burden

I am not my brother's keeper.

—Mark

O ne of the humorous times in raising my toddler twins was
when they began to use language effectively. Around the
age of twenty-one months, they were starting to master
one-word identification to great effect. Each swiftly learned how
to direct undesirable parent behavior toward her sister. For instance, the morning routine began with diaper changing, and if I
moved toward Tal to change her diaper, she'd point to her sister
and say, "Eden." I would ask, "Should I change Eden's diaper
first?" and she would nod yes. My husband and I would laugh

when it was apparent that one child was "selling the other out." That, to us, was a sign of a healthy sibling relationship!

Still, more often than not, I see that they tend to take care of each other rather than throw each other under the bus. My heart has melted when observing one toddler walking across the room to grab a pacifier to hand to her crying sister. I relished the thought that my children were developing a strong sense of empathy—something I so wanted them to possess but didn't necessarily know how to impart upon them.

Yet I knew that I didn't want each of them to feel solely, or even mostly, responsible for the emotional well-being of the other. And I wasn't sure how to balance encouraging empathy for one another and imposing responsibility for the other's emotional well-being. In fact, I'm still not sure.

Dr. Joan Friedman wrote of her experience growing up as a twin:

> From a young age, I suffered because I felt it was my responsibility as Jane's twin to make sure she was happy and comfortable. Worrying that my actions, and even my feelings, might make her unhappy depleted my energy and held me back from discovering who I was. I often felt sad because it was so hard to be an authentic, separate person who could do, say, and be whatever I wanted without feeling pressured to consider the effects on Jane.[1]

Of the twins I interviewed, there was a similar description of the acute awareness of one's actions affecting one's twin, but it was not always considered negative or unfortunate. Many of the twins felt perfectly at peace with feeling that way, especially because the feeling was often reciprocated.

A good number of the twins I interviewed valued that close emotional relationship they shared with their twin siblings. They felt safe and secure knowing that someone else on the planet knew, cared for, and loved them so deeply.

In some cases, however, the feeling of responsibility was not perfectly mutual and reciprocal. In some twin couplets, one of the twins felt comforted by the close emotional bond and one of the twins felt somewhat burdened by it. The latter group felt that they needed more space and didn't like feeling responsible for their twin's safety, well-being, and social needs, similar to the sentiment expressed by Dr. Friedman. And while some twins didn't mind being a caretaker at times, they did mind the constant assumption that they were the caretakers for their twin siblings in every single circumstance. This was a particularly poignant sentiment in the case of social settings. One twin felt burdened by always having to bring along his twin sister or worrying about the repercussions if he decided to hang out with friends without her. In Chapter Eight, I will discuss the dynamic in which one twin felt responsible for his co-twin in social settings and how that sense of responsibility tainted his own experience making (and keeping) friends.

Triplet Mark explained that, in middle school, he was once invited to attend a weekend getaway with a friend, and his mother forbade him from going. The host was a mutual friend of all three triplets, but he invited only Mark. Mark's mother was concerned that the other two brothers would be hurt to learn that only Mark was invited. So Mark had to discreetly decline, and his brothers never learned of the invitation.

Sometimes loyalty is forced upon children by parents, as with Mark, and sometimes twins feel a sense of duty on their own. Many twins I interviewed felt personally blameworthy when their twin siblings misbehaved. A twin child often would observe the inappropriate behavior but feel unable to speak out against the behavior for fear of being perceived as disloyal. And while she may not have engaged in the misbehavior directly, the observing twin would either directly confess to the rule-breaking or at least not deny her role in it. She would often feel connected to the misbehavior simply by being the twin of the wrongdoer. Parents tend to reinforce this personal feeling of guilt for poor behavior by imposing the same penalty on each child, even in instances where the parent knows that only one of the children committed the offending act.

Another example of twins feeling responsible for each other's actions came from Amanda, in a story involving her sister Jill. Amanda recalls when she and Jill were five years old and went shopping in a department store with their mother.

"We were walking through racks of clothes, like an endless maze to a tiny five-year-old, when Jill was suddenly gone," Amanda said. "She had been walking right behind me. Mom and I had no idea where she went. I was horrified."

Their mom called for Jill and found her behind a

> When my daughters were four years old, I realized that I must have been exclaiming "Damn it!" within their earshot. I would hear Tal challenging me with "Oh damage!" when she was testing the boundaries of acceptable language. I remember driving in the car with the girls in their car seats behind me. Tal said loudly, "Damage!"
>
> I pulled the car over so I could turn around and look at her. Feigning disappointment, I said, "What was that, Tal?"
>
> Silence.
>
> I asked again: "Tal—What. Did. You. Say?"
>
> Silence.
>
> "Tell me!"
>
> And then Eden—with wide, fearful eyes—slowly whispered, "She said 'damage.'"

nearby rack. She was missing for maybe twenty seconds—but it felt like an eternity to Amanda.

"I was crying more than Jill was when we found her," Amanda said.

The language Amanda used to describe that brief but terrifying moment—"I felt guilty that I lost her"—fascinated me. She was five years old, and with her mother, and yet it was *she* who felt personally responsible for having lost Jill. Rather than recognizing that her mother—the adult—was responsible, Amanda just internalized the blame and guilt. This sense of personal responsibility for the whereabouts, well-being, and safety of one's twin was common among the twins I interviewed.

A 2016 *Guardian* article featured identical twins Richard and Antony. At age fourteen, Antony was diagnosed with cancer and had to undergo grueling treatments. Richard recalled, "It was excruciating being forced apart when [Antony] was in the hospital—I'd sleep in his bed—but the hardest thing was watching it all happen, being on the periphery and feeling helpless. . . . I went through a range of emotions. *Why him and not me?* was on my mind a lot. The guilt was crushing. I ended up having counseling in my twenties and thirties, to try to cope with it. I'm still not sure I've recovered."[2]

In another example, twin interviewees Ethan and Randall were very different from each other. Ethan was an "overachiever" and "one of the smartest kids in the class." Randall, on the other hand, had dyslexia and saw that there was no way he could beat Ethan for their father's approval, so he decided to "compete for negative attention."

"I was always getting in trouble, but it was out of frustration," Randall said. "I often would run away from home. Ethan was the one who would always find me. He just knew where I would go. Now, I look back on it and I feel bad because I worried Ethan.

That's why he always was the one to find me. He was worried about me."

Randall also said that if he was in a fight in the school yard, Ethan would show up "with impeccable timing." Randall remarked, "I don't know how he knew, but Ethan just always knew [something was about to go down] . . . and he would always show up at exactly the right time."

When I spoke with Ethan separately, he confirmed that he was often worried about Randall when they were growing up, and even as adults, he does what he can to help him. Ethan did not express resentment about always being there to support Randall, and he seemed to feel that his actions were no more special than anyone else who wants to help take care of family.

I was touched by former President Bill Clinton's book *My Life* when reading about his sense of duty in caring for his younger brother Roger. When Bill Clinton was fourteen years old and his brother Roger was four, their abusive father (Roger's biological father; Bill's stepfather) was once again screaming at their mother. What inspired Clinton to break open his parents' bedroom door to intervene was that he "couldn't bear the thought of Mother being hurt and Roger being frightened."[3] He was willing to put himself at risk of bodily harm to save his mother from physical injury and his brother from emotional injury.

Later in his biography, Clinton describes how he felt when he learned that Roger had been videotaped selling cocaine to an undercover police officer. He explained, "Every time I looked in the mirror I was disgusted. I had been so caught up in my life and work that I'd missed all the signs. . . . The warning signs were all there. I was just too preoccupied to see them."[4]

At the time of Roger's arrest, Bill was the governor of Arkansas, and instead of expressing embarrassment or frustration at having to deal with the public relations nightmare,

Clinton's primary focus was on what he perceived to be his grave omissions as a brother. Clinton's concern was not about the political repercussions this incident would impose but instead about how self-centered he felt he was and how he might have been able to intervene and help his struggling, drug-addicted brother—if he had only paid more attention to him and less attention to his own career and life.

And while Bill and Roger Clinton are not twins, they are brothers. Bill, as the older sibling, felt (and probably still feels) a deep sense of responsibility not only for the well-being of his brother but also for the choices his brother makes for himself as a grown adult.

Some twin interviewees expressed feelings of guilt when they wanted to go to a different camp, take a different extracurricular class, or, in adolescent and teenage years, apply to different academic summer programs or universities. This was particularly prevalent in relationships where one twin felt more like an older sibling with very specific caretaker responsibilities for the other. In these cases, the twin who desired the different opportunity felt guilty "leaving his brother behind." Reactions to this instinct ranged from some twins avoiding any guilty feelings by not trying to pursue the solo adventure to others who pursued the activity but felt guilty for doing so. Contrast this phenomenon with the experience of a singleton who typically does not need to gauge the joy or sadness of a sibling when weighing his options for academic or extracurricular pursuits.

Many individuals I interviewed felt personally responsible for the shortcomings or failures of their twin siblings, which weighed heavily on their minds and caused them stress. In a child's lifetime, there are ample events that can set her up for success or failure: auditions for school plays, tryouts for sports teams, and applications to academic programs or college. When these opportunities are pursued by both twins, there is a strong chance that awkward and painful moments will arise in which one twin succeeds and the other does not. The successful child's joy is often tempered by the disappointment she feels that her twin did not achieve the same success.

As we will discuss in Chapter Six, parents should make concerted efforts to not compare their twin children to each other. The twins should not feel that they need to define themselves by how they compare to one another. Parents should reduce, as much as possible, the competition that may exist between their twin children. But to the extent that there is competition between them (Indeed, how can there be none at all?), each child should feel proud to celebrate his accomplishments without fear that doing so will upset his twin. Parents should encourage a healthy sense of self-esteem in each child so that each child could feel proud of, and happy for, his twin's successes. Note that giving specific praise in moments of success will also help the recipient of the compliment feel that you are being sincere. Experts note that vague praise ("Way to go!") has far less positive impact than specific praise ("You worked really hard to master your handwriting, and the hard work paid off! Your handwriting is very clear and legible!").

Twins with a tight emotional bond tend to feel the physical and emotional pain that their twin siblings experience more acutely than in the typical sibling relationship. As discussed in Chapter One, grieving for the loss of life or one's parents' marriage seems more manageable when it is a shared experience. In cases where one twin suffers her own personal loss (such as the death of an in-law, child, or spouse), the other twin sibling tends to acutely feel the pain that her sibling feels, which in turn deepens the individual's ability to empathize with her suffering sibling in a way that no other family member or friend could.

# Intervening (in Love and in War)

While twin interviewees thought parents should encourage twins to feel close to each other, they also felt that parents should step back and allow the children to control how close they wanted to be. If they ask to be separated, allow them to have that space. Let your children guide you through how much separation they want and need. If your children are not forthcoming with those feelings, at the very least, take cues from them. Of course, it makes a parent's job increasingly difficult when one twin child seems to want separation more than the other. The parent will have to figure out a workable way of balancing one twin's needs with the other's and make a determination as to which path will allow the twin children to form a healthy bond.

Parents should explain to children that the twin bond is unique and special but that it's okay to sometimes wish one wasn't a twin. It's okay to sometimes feel resentful toward one's twin sibling. It's okay to want to explore one's own individual identity. It's okay to want alone time. Feelings of frustration about being a twin are normal, and children should feel free to express those feelings without feeling guilty for having them. As one interviewee put it, "I just wanted my parents to recognize that being a twin wasn't always the best thing in the world."

A twin interviewee who is in an interracial marriage reads his children books that deal gently with issues interracial children may face. He wants to make sure his children feel okay with their differences and that they are prepared for societal or social challenges with which they may be confronted. He suggested that parents approach raising twin children with the same sensitivity to their unique circumstances: read them books that address topics to which the twins can relate, and talk to them about challenges that may arise—challenges imposed on them by society or that organically arise from the unique twin relationship itself.

And while some parents are very good at "talking to" their children, it is imperative that parents give their child a chance to talk. Parents should ensure that their children feel heard. I love that the words *listen* and *silent* share the same letters. In order to really listen, parents have to be silent and allow their child to talk. Resist the temptation to say "Uh-huh" or "Right" in response to every point made by the child; a simple and quiet nod of the head with good eye contact will indicate that you are listening. By interrupting your child with your verbal affirmations, you risk silencing the child. Quiet space in between sentences could encourage your child to continue opening up (a helpful tip from when I used to practice law: witnesses feel compelled to fill the silence with words and may give you the information you really need without you having to even ask the question!). And for smaller children, parents may want to sit on the floor or adjust their position so they are at eye level with their child. Ensure that your body language is open as well. Crossed arms in front of your chest, for instance, might inaccurately convey that you are angry, anxious, closed off, controlling, or defensive, whereas an open posture could indicate that you are collaborative, friendly, peaceful, and willing to listen.

Experienced parents will often advise newer parents to let their children "work it out" themselves when engaging in a conflict. This sage advice is no different for parents of twin children. Indeed, with twin children there are generally more opportunities for sibling conflict than with children of different ages, as twin children are more often competing for the same toys, resources, and attention. The exception to the "no intervention" rule is when one child is at risk for causing significant physical injury to the other child. Generally, children should be taught how to deal constructively with their own anger and to not resort to violent behaviors.

A parent may be tempted to intervene in a fight between their twin children because they want their children to be close friends at all times. Parents should rest assured that even though they fight, close friends with a healthy relationship will never "break up."

Of course, parental duties do not cease to be important when twins are peaceful with, and emotionally close to, each other. When parents observe a very close emotional relationship between their twin children, they should take special note if the dynamic is more akin to parent-child than child-child. While being empathic and caring for each other is healthy, one child should not constantly take on a caregiving or parental role for the other. Such behavior could be a sign that the parents are not providing enough emotional support to the children. In that case, the parents should make overt efforts to welcome their children to come to them in times of emotional need, and they should reiterate that their job as parents is to make the children feel better in difficult times.

## Balancing Empathy and the Burden of Caregiving

When my children were about fifteen months old, Tal caught some sort of illness that caused her to incessantly cough throughout the night. I listened to and watched a live video feed of her through a monitor; I could see her body tossing and turning as she tried to find comfort. At around 3:00 a.m., Tal finally stopped coughing. She was exhausted and fell into a deep sleep. Once I confirmed, through observing her belly rise and fall rhythmically, that she was asleep, I closed my eyes, rolled back, and allowed myself to also drift to sleep . . . until about 3:45 a.m., when I awoke to the sound of Eden, who shared a room with Tal, wailing loudly.

I rolled quickly out of bed and ran down the hallway to their room. I swept in, grabbed Eden out of her crib, and ran down the hallway to a point where I felt certain that Tal would not hear Eden's crying.

My own heart was racing; I felt as if I would do anything to not wake up Tal, who so desperately needed to sleep.

I hissed at Eden, "Shhhhh! Don't wake up Tal! You cannot scream like that. Tal is sick and needs her sleep."

I helped Eden calm down with some deep breathing techniques, but as she started to relax, I realized that I had made a sizable mistake: Eden had screamed because she had a bad dream (I think) and needed to be comforted by me. The fact that Tal was sick was of no consequence to Eden at that moment.

I thought to myself, *If Eden had been a singleton, I would have picked her up and instantly soothed her. The first words out of my mouth would have been ones of comfort.* Instead, my first words were harsh and accusatory; they failed to address Eden's condition and instead were focused on Tal's needs. While it's good for Eden to learn to be conscious and considerate of those around her, she had her own very significant needs in this instance. Why should I diminish her desire for comfort and soothing, and essentially ignore her needs, simply because there was a sleeping child in her room at the time?

I was wrong to impose a caretaking burden on Eden. I should not have showed her that I expected her to suppress her own needs in favor of her sister's needs. And I was wrong as well to not validate Eden's feelings; validation of feelings is an important step in showing your children that you understand them and that it's okay to feel what they're feeling. (This was clearly not one of my finer parenting moments.)

But is a child never to consider how her actions affect her twin sibling? Don't we want our children to be empathic and have concern for others, especially others in their own family? How, then, does a parent find the balance between their child having empathy for others and not feeling inappropriately burdened by caretaking responsibilities for them?

I am not entirely certain that there is a hard and fast rule for this—I surmise that the line would rest in a different place depending on the varying personalities of the children involved.

In my case, in the above scenario, I should have made it my first priority to immediately soothe Eden. That might result in her crying a little more or explaining to me in a loud voice what was upsetting her. If that woke up Tal, so be it. I cannot expect Eden to be empathic in the middle of the night when all she can focus on is whatever is ailing her and her need to be heard and soothed. While it wouldn't hurt for her to understand that her sounds woke up Mommy and Tal (and possibly the neighbors!), she should not be admonished for, or made to feel guilty about, this unfortunate chain reaction.

Even if I had reacted perfectly in that situation, and in the many others that were presented to me, it still wouldn't guarantee that my twins would develop a completely healthy relationship full of empathy and without undue caretaking burdens. So what if, despite your best efforts, one child seems to assume responsibility for his co-twin? What if you witness him suppressing his own significant needs in order to take care of his co-twin?

It may help to explain to him that your job as his parent is to take care of both of them, that you take that job very seriously, and that you will try your best at all times to do so. You may enlist his help in caring for his twin ("Could you grab that cup of water and we can give it to your sister?"), but the message should be that you, as the parent, are ultimately responsible for the well-being of each child.

And what if, despite your best efforts, one child seems to be totally indifferent to the needs of his co-twin? What if you find no element of empathy in his actions toward his co-twin? You may have to teach empathy in small, manageable doses. When your child is upset, help him identify the cause of his distress; use your words to dictate what you observed and see if he can verify that what you sense is correct. Eventually, he will be able to use his own words to express his feelings. Whenever you hear or see another child crying, you could ask your child why he thinks the child is crying. You could enlist your child's help in caring for his co-twin ("Do you see that your brother's nose is running? Maybe that feels uncomfortable. Should we bring him a tissue?"). Even better, ask your child to identify and then help solve the problem ("Why do you think your sister is crying? What can we do to help her feel better?"). Remember to consistently praise the child for his acts of empathy so you are reinforcing the good behavior. Most importantly, *you* must be empathic toward others. Children learn from the modeling that you do, so be caring toward other people, and your children will learn to be caring toward others too.

Empathy and kindness are really important values in my house. We try to make sure our home is a cruelty-free zone; we consume only vegan products and personally escort spiders out the door (with the help of a postcard and plastic cup). And while talking meanly about someone behind her back and other rude social gestures are discouraged, I also want to find a balance that enables a kid to be a kid. If that means singing a funny song about poop or making fun of a family member for making a silly mistake, we make some allowances for what wouldn't otherwise be our best "in public" behavior.

We can easily usurp so much joy in childhood by imposing rigid rules or strict household mores. Empathy toward others is important, but so is enjoying one's childhood. Jennifer Senior aptly notes what is so beneficial about being near children—why we consider them to be our "bundles of joy":

> It's not just because they're soft and sweet and smell like perfection. They also create wormholes in time, transporting their mothers and fathers back to feelings and sensations they haven't had since they themselves were young. . . . [All] of us crave liberation from our adult selves, at least from time to time. I'm not just talking about the selves with public roles to play and daily obligations to meet. . . . I'm talking about the selves who live too much in their heads rather than their bodies; who are burdened with too much knowledge about how the world works rather than excited by how it could work or should; who are afraid of being judged and not being loved. Most adults do not live in a world of forgiveness and unconditional love. Unless, that is, they have small children.[5]

Caretaking is a heavy burden. Why impose that upon a child whose job description is more about running after butterflies and giggling at funny-sounding words? Empathy is an important value to teach, but we should teach it in fun ways, lead by example, and show that it's the kind of thing we do because doing for others simply feels good.

# Tips for Reducing the Caretaker Burden

- Make sure you are giving each child adequate emotional support so that she knows that she can rely on you, and not her twin, to parent her.

- Find ways to give space to each child.
- Acknowledge that it may be frustrating at times to be a twin and that it's okay to have conflicting feelings about it.
- Encourage each child to succeed (and, yes, fail) on his own and digest the outcome with the child individually, outside of the presence of his twin.
- Do not punish both children for the actions of one child.
- Encourage each child to develop her own friends separate from those of her twin.
- Support your children's desires to socialize in different crowds, and do not force one child to bring his twin sibling along.
- Do not make one child the responsibility of the other. Avoid phrases like "Look after your sister" or "Don't let your brother hurt himself" or "Aren't you taking your sister along?"
- Celebrate the success of each child with that child individually. Give praise that speaks to the specific qualities of the child.
- Remind your children that it is your job (not theirs) to take care of both children.
- It's okay for your child to learn that his actions affect others, but do not make him feel guilty for simply expressing his needs, even when that expression may have negative consequences for others.
- If you see a lack of compassion in one child, teach her empathy by helping her identify feelings and how to help soothe others.
- Teach your child empathy for all; do not impose the need for him to empathize disproportionately with his co-twin.

- Positively reinforce good, empathic behavior with gratitude and praise.
- Model good behavior; be compassionate toward others.
- Encourage each child to pursue his own interests without deep concern for how that pursuit will affect his twin sibling.
- Positively reinforce behaviors that demonstrate a close, mutually supportive bond while discouraging behaviors that demonstrate one twin's absorption of the other twin's failures, losses, or misbehavior.

1. Friedman, *Emotionally Healthy Twins*, 1.

2. Pook, "'I've Never Needed Anyone Else'."

3. Bill Clinton, *My Life: The Early Years* (New York: Vintage Books, 2005), 58.

4. Ibid, 415.

5. Senior, *All Joy and No Fun*, 98–9.

# CHAPTER FOUR

# One-On-One Time Is More Important Than You Think

*I never had a meal alone with my parents.*

—Almost all twin interviewees

**D**uring my interviews, I always asked my subjects what they wished their parents did differently in raising them. One answer seemed to continuously come up, even for those (and there were a lot!) who thought their parents did a great job raising them.

"More one-on-one time," they universally replied.

When my children turned one year old, I started scheduling my daughters' doctor's appointments on separate days. This was something I probably should have done sooner—I notice the doctor's attention is more focused and less hurried when there is only one child in the room. Each child then receives better medical care. It also makes it easier for me to soothe the child who receives shots or other invasive procedures because she is the sole recipient of my care. But the added bonus to single doctor visits was that I would have some cherished one-on-one time with the child in the car, in the waiting room, and for a special post-visit treat (like a quick trip to the playground) to reward the child for her courage. I think these one-on-one post-doctor dates were the silver lining to the otherwise dark cloud of doctor visits; any fear the child had seemed to be outweighed by the privilege of one hundred percent of Mommy's attention (and getting to choose what music we listened to in the car!).

They would have liked more time with their parents without their twin or any other sibling. And while this sentiment tended to ring true for spending alone time with non-parental family members, such as other siblings, cousins, and grandparents, the answer, more often than not, was specific to one-on-one time with parents.

In a mindful parenting course I attended, we were asked to reflect on our own childhoods and describe what we wished our parents had done differently in raising us. One participant noted that she was a child in a large family of nine siblings. Her main complaint about her childhood was that she felt that she and her siblings were not distinguished and recognized for their unique qualities. "I would have liked it if my parents spent more time getting to know each of us individually," she added, "rather than just grouping us as 'one of the kids.'" And while large families are not necessarily the norm, this woman's reflection revealed that the feeling of being just an item in a group is not a feeling reserved exclusively for twins.

Still, there's a significantly higher likelihood that a twin would feel a more urgent need to be recognized as a unique individual. And to meet that need, parents of those children need to spend more alone time getting to know them.

My children were about sixteen months old when I noticed the prevalence of this desire for more one-on-one time among my interviewees. I made a personal vow that I would make weekly one-on-one dates with each of my twin children. Some weeks, my husband and children and I would pile into the car. I'd drop him and one child off at a local bagel shop while I took the other to the market to shop for groceries. I'd then pick them back up and we'd all go to the playground together. Or sometimes we'd each take a child to separate playgrounds. Other times, when my husband's schedule didn't give him much time with us on the weekends, I would enlist the help of a family member or babysitter to stay with one child while I took the other one somewhere—anywhere. I tried to switch up whom I took and whom I left behind as consistently as possible so no child felt denied the special "Mommy time."

After some time, I found that making weekly one-on-one dates with each child was excellent in theory but flawed in practicality. I couldn't always find someone to help out, and my husband would often discourage one-on-one dates during the weekends, stating that he missed the girls all week and just wanted to "be together as a family." Sometimes, multiple weeks would go by without one-on-one time. Naturally, I felt guilty with every passing week that the girls didn't receive their special alone time, but I had to face the reality that logistics and personal stress will sometimes undo my otherwise good intentions.

What I did find, however, was that any time I felt that one child was acting up—being fussy, whiny, difficult, impossible to please—a simple antidote of alone time was often all it took to restore good behavior.

Clinical psychologist and creator of the *Aha! Parenting* website Dr. Laura Markham often associates poor behavior of children with the lack of feeling connected to their parents.[1] This theory has proven very true for us. If we have a busy weekend of playdates and celebrations with relatives, often by the end of the weekend, at least one child will be difficult to please or will engage in antisocial behaviors. I am very diligent about ensuring that my children maintain as normal a sleeping and eating routine as possible to obviate possible meltdowns; I thus could not simply point to hunger or fatigue as the cause of the unseemly behavior. What I've found is that the cause of this poor behavior is a feeling of disconnect or distance from me.

For example, after a long week of preschool, evening playdates and activities, and then an entire day with cousins, my twenty-month-old daughter started crying every time her cousin went to sit in the red patio chair she liked. This was very atypical behavior for the child who is usually very easygoing and generous. I extracted her from the scene and took her to another room where we hugged, cuddled, and sang songs. Within minutes, I could see her foul mood dissipate. We spent a total of ten minutes alone with each other, and she returned to the patio with an uplifted spirit and eager willingness to share.

In *Raising Resilient Children: Fostering Strength, Hope, and Optimism in Your Child*, Robert Brooks, PhD, and Sam Goldstein, PhD, write that alone time with a child is essential to helping him develop into a resilient adult.[2] Many parents mistakenly fear that by showing their child too much love, they'll spoil him. When my daughters were newborns, a well-meaning older family member told me not to rush to comfort a crying baby, lest I spoil her; I should let her cry so she can grow accustomed to the uncomfortable feeling of not getting what she wants all the time. Thankfully, I did not heed that particular relative's advice. I did rush to soothe my crying babies, and I can tell you with confidence that today, they are not spoiled.

Contrary to some more ancient ways of thinking, Brooks and Goldstein state that children who feel loved by their parents are more receptive to accepting limits and taking responsibility; they also tend to show more empathy toward others. And a crucial way to make your children feel loved is to allot special alone time for them. Brooks and Goldstein suggest that alone time with your child should be part of a tradition that you create: a time that is set aside each day, week, or month as special time. By designating the ritual as *special time*, "we convey the message to our children that they are important to us and that we enjoy having uninterrupted time to spend with them."

It is imperative for parents to adhere to and respect these designated times as they might a business meeting—cancel or postpone only in the case of an exigent and unavoidable circumstance. Too many cancellations, and your boss will get the impression that you're not serious about the job. So, too, with your children. If you are frequently missing special time with them, they will start to doubt the extent of your love and respect for them.

Many twin interviewees commented that they could not recall having one meal alone with their parent(s). In their entire lives, not one meal! This sentiment sounded hyperbolic to me until I thought back and realized that my toddler-aged children had

Sometimes two-on-one time happens organically, without intention—lean into those remarkable experiences! I recall a Sunday morning when our intention was to let the kids, then three years old, sleep in after an active and exciting Saturday evening. Thanks to recently switching our clocks for Daylight Savings Time, Eden was awake at 6:00 a.m. We didn't want her to wake up Tal, so we brought her into bed with us. She couldn't sleep, so she began to talk. And talk. And talk. We had never before heard so many words and so many coherent sentences come out of her mouth. It turns out, she had a lot of thoughts about a lot of things, and finally she could tell us everything all at once! We propped ourselves up on our pillows and smiled widely as our daughter demonstrated her articulateness, thought processes, and overwhelming desire to talk without interruption—and without her sister looming nearby. How rarely did she enjoy undivided attention from both parents!

never had one sit-down meal alone with either (or both) of their parents. I then envisioned how enjoyable that would be and made another personal vow to make this happen.

So, with my new goal in mind, I dropped one child off at a friend's house and took the other to a local coffee shop. It felt like a naughty adventure, one that we should keep secret. It was just so novel and enjoyable that it felt like it must be sinful in some way! I began to make this activity a regular adventure: I made it a habit to drop one child off at a playdate while I took the other for a special treat at the local bakery. The playdate was much easier for the hosting parent, the hosting child had special one-on-one time with one child, and the child I took to the bakery and I enjoyed alone time together. It was a win-win-win-win!

The general theme of this chapter is one-on-one time, but I would urge parents who have a caretaking partner to attempt an even loftier and logistically more difficult goal: two-on-one time. A first-born singleton raised in a two-parent household can typically recollect fond memories when she was taken to the playground or to a museum or to a community event with both parents. In fact, it's a common scene at a playground on the weekend to see two parents taking photos and marveling at the milestones of their only child as she grows. But many adult twins cannot recall a time when they ever had one hundred percent of *both* parents' attention. Ever!

I recall when my twin daughter Eden was almost two years old and started screaming in the middle of the night. My husband and I rushed in to pick her up so she wouldn't wake up Tal, with whom she shared a room. We brought Eden to the bathroom so we could turn on the light and figure out what was wrong. I sat at the edge of the bathtub with Eden on my lap, and my husband turned on the light. The moment she saw that she had both of us there with her, she calmed down. At first, she asked for a tissue to wipe her nose. Then she asked for medicine to soothe her tooth pain. Then she asked for us to take her socks off. And then put them back on. When she had seemingly exhausted all possible requests, I stood up to take her back to her crib and she started crying again. When we asked what was wrong, she smiled and shrugged. There was nothing left; we concluded that she was just enjoying the very special two-on-one time and didn't want it to end.

The most important piece of advice to achieve one-on-one time and two-on-one time (arguably the most difficult to implement) is this: enlist help. How special it would be for a grandparent to have alone time with one of your twin children so you can have special time with the other! Then switch! Caretakers, relatives, and your partner will enjoy an "easy" childcare experience with just

Do you have relatives in a different state? It might make sense to schedule time to visit your relatives with one of your children. One twin interviewee mentioned that his mother would take one child to another state to visit her mother for an entire weekend, and she would alternate whom she took with every visit. He recalled this memory fondly as a time in which he bonded with his mother.

one child while you can enjoy time with the other child. If you must hire a babysitter whom you have to pay, do so! Even if all you want to pay for is an hour once a week (or, more practically speaking, a two- or three-hour session every two to three weeks), do so. In the short term, it may feel like an added investment for which you hadn't previously budgeted, but in the long run, it will pay off. After all, when your children are older, you won't remember the restaurant meal or purse you couldn't afford because you spent that money on a babysitter, but you (and your child) will most likely remember the time you and he took a special one-on-one outing to the playground, where you slid with him down slides or helped him hone his throwing and catching skills.

Imagine what it might be like for a three-year-old child who has had less than her parents' full attention since she was born to have an entire day devoted to her wants and needs. She could wake up when her circadian rhythms dictate as opposed to the time when her sister wakes her up. She could eat what she wanted, when she wanted, without having the dietary habits and needs of her twin sister taken into consideration. She could use the bathroom when she wanted. She could sit in any chair at the kitchen table. She could choose which playground to attend. The possibilities for empowerment and independence are limitless!

Now imagine the twin adolescent who has the focused attention of both parents at the same time, without the presence of her sister: she could choose the music in the car and the show on the television. She could individually choose where she would like to shop for clothes. She could ask her parents a question and reasonably expect a prompt answer. She may miss her twin sister and she may not, but one thing is certain: you will have given her an opportunity to feel like her parents' only child, at least for a delicious moment in time.

Adolescents, in particular, have a special need to talk with parents as they experience rapid physical and emotional changes. They are in dire need of parental guidance during the roller coaster ride of changing hormones, increased social tensions, and heightened academic pressure. This is a time in your adolescents' lives when they might need more one-on-one time. Even if you can give that one-on-one time only in short bursts, it would be wise to prioritize the endeavor so that at the very least, you are checking in with each child weekly, in private, and opening the doors of free, uninhibited communication.

Some twin interviewees mentioned that alone time with a parent during the middle and high school years would have made those challenging times easier. Other twins who had that one-on-one time felt grateful for those moments.

There are many simple ways parents of twins can create one-on-one or two-on-one time. Here are some examples:

- A close friend of mine has four kids. There's no way she can give each child the attention he craves at all times. For their respective birthdays, she takes the birthday child out of school for the day and has a Mom-and-Kid Day. They do something special that the child would like: go to an arcade, see a movie, go to the playground, play soccer in the backyard, have a meal at his favorite

When my children were toddlers, I would bathe them together at the same time. I have many cute videos of them pouring water over each other's legs with plastic mini watering cans and of them singing songs off key. But bath time seemed to always take a turn within about five minutes—Tal would slap her hands down on the water, splashing Eden, and Eden would immediately start to cry and ask to be taken out of the tub. I would diaper and dress Eden in the bathroom while Tal continued to enjoy her bath. In fact, Tal never seemed to want bath time to be over. I assumed Tal liked being in the water more and Eden maybe felt safer out of the tub. One night, my husband had a one-on-one date with Tal and I had a one-on-one date with Eden. By the time Eden and I had arrived home, Tal had already finished her bath. I bathed Eden alone and was tickled to see her enjoying it! She played with all the toys and traveled from one end of the tub to another, trying out different postures and positions in the tub. After fifteen minutes and impressively pruned skin, she was still having fun, and I tempered my usually impatient tendencies to allow her to revel in the aloneness of this bath experience. It turns out she did not dislike baths; to the contrary, she loved baths—she just disliked sharing them.

restaurant, and enjoy quality time together. Consider doing a version of this with your own children. At least once a year, maybe near the child's birthday, take one child out of school for the day and spend the entire day with him, doing what he would like. Make sure your day with the other child follows not too long after. Some

parents might bristle at this idea—it requires taking
a day off from work and taking a child out of school.
Again, I urge the reader to weigh the long-term benefits
with the short-term risks. It's two total vacation days
that you are losing, but the benefit to your relationship
with your child—and to his self-esteem—is invaluable.
If it is too challenging to schedule this event, consider
enlisting help so your child can have the special day over
the weekend or whenever you are not working.

- While regular half-day or full-day one-on-one dates
  with each child are ideal, as mentioned, even short, regular bursts of alone time would go a long way in making
  each child feel special. Try to find moments (no matter
  how finite) throughout the day or week when you can
  have some one-on-one time with a child. If one child is
  occupied by a toy or a book, give the other child a quick
  hug and see what activity he would like to do with you.
  His sibling may quickly join in, but you shared a little
  moment when you and he hugged and communicated
  with each other.

- If you don't mind giving up the precious alone time
  you have as a parent while your children nap, have the
  twins nap at different times so you can have some alone
  time with the non-napping child. I admit that I never
  did this, because I felt that I needed my children's joint
  naptime to accomplish household tasks. In retrospect,
  I realize that I probably could have figured out a way to
  cook or clean another time—or to skip it and not let that
  bother me. After all, no one ever says on her deathbed
  that she wishes she had spent more time cooking and
  cleaning!

- If one teenager is engaged in a schoolwork obligation or on the phone, try to engage her twin in a dialogue about school or friends or a movie. It may not be "alone time" per se, because the other child is nearby, but it certainly helps give one child more focused attention.

- Walk and talk (with one at a time). One twin reported that her mother would go for a walk after dinner with either her or her twin brother, alternating which child she took every other night. This enabled the child with the focused attention to talk freely with her mother without having to balance concerns about sharing certain information in front of her twin sibling.

Small gestures like that add up. As author Stephen Covey explains in *The 7 Habits of Highly Effective Families*, healthy relationships develop from putting effective deposits into the "emotional bank account"—a metaphor describing the collection of trust and security among the proverbial owners of the account.[3] The richer the account, the safer the individuals feel with each other in the relationship. By making small but frequent gestures toward one-on-one time with your child, you are depositing into that emotional bank account and making it richer and fuller while helping your child feel safer in the relationship.

It is also important for parents to look at how communication works in their household, and they should seek to foster an open line of communication among all family members. This may not be a way of directly creating one-on-one or two-on-one time, but it does make those times more productive if a child feels able to share freely. Does each child feel comfortable expressing his feelings without fear of being ignored, judged, or punished? How well do you listen to your children? When young children talk incessantly about seemingly mundane events that happened at school that day, do you listen or are you more prone to tune it out? If a preschooler is accustomed to you not listening, what makes you think she'll disclose any information to you when she's an adolescent?

In order to encourage open dialogue with your children, parents need to be trustworthy. They need to generally keep private information confidential and tell the truth. Do you lie a lot to your children? Do you tell them that the shot at the doctor's office is not going to hurt when you know it will? How often do you put your young child in a position to question your sincerity? The more frequently she discovers that you were not honest, the less likely she is to trust you as time passes. A parent should not want a child of any age to question her trustworthiness. In most, if not all, cases, it is in everyone's best interests if you tell the truth.

Along with trust and open communication, it is important that we have focused time with our children. Some of us well-meaning parents think that spending *more* time with our children is the antidote to a feeling of disconnect from them. We work long hours, and when we're at work, we feel guilty for not being with our children. We tell ourselves that we are at work *for them*, that we need to work this many hours in order to give them a life that they deserve, to give them things and opportunities we never had. We have photos of them on our desks, and we spend a portion of our lunch breaks watching videos of them on our phones. Gazing at their images and thinking about them somehow lifts the heavy veil of guilt, but only slightly—we know deep in our hearts that we would feel like better parents if we were with them in person.

But if someone were to ask our kids whether they wanted or needed more time with us, we might be surprised to learn their answer. Ellen Galinsky, leading authority on work-family issues and cofounder of Families and Work Institute, conducted a study of more than one thousand children ranging from ages eight to eighteen. She asked the children how they would change the way their mother's and father's work affected their lives. The results are featured in her book *Ask the Children: What America's Children Really Think about Working Parents*. Only 10 percent said they wished they had more time with their mothers. A whopping 34 percent, however, said they wished their mothers were "less tired" and "less stressed." The proportions for fathers were similar: 15 percent wished they had more time with their fathers, while 27.5 percent wished their fathers were less tired and stressed.[4] So while we feel bad that we are not always physically present with our children, what they really want from us is not more time with our bodies but more time with our brains, our thoughts, our feelings, our hearts. They don't want more of our hours; they want more of our energy, our creativity, our goodwill, our sense of humor, and our positivity.

I urge the reader to consider the finiteness of time and the quality of the little time we have on this earth with our children—at the age that they are today and the age that they'll be when time has flown to twenty years from now. Don't miss out on moments. Turn off the television. Put the smartphone down. Tell the guests to leave the house. Look your children in the eyes and connect with them. Time is fleeting. Don't waste it.

# Tips for Making On-on-One Time Happen

- Schedule separate doctor's appointments for each child.
- Make one-on-one times part of a weekly tradition—even if the one-on-one time is one to two hours at a time.
- Have regular conversations with each child alone, without the other present.

- Enlist help!
- Encourage one-on-one time with your children and relatives and/or caretakers.
- Consider taking one child out of school for one day and then alternating (on a relatively infrequent basis).
- Stay connected with each child. Sometimes all it takes to restore the connection is ten to twenty minutes of focused attention, play, or cuddling (age will likely determine which of those bonding activities you pursue).
- For coupled parents, at least once or twice a year, try to arrange a two-on-one date with one child, then alternate children.
- Small but frequent gestures go a long way—do not decide against a moment of one-on-one time simply because it seems short.
- Tell your children that you understand that they are in a unique situation and that it can be frustrating to not have one hundred percent of a parent's attention or to always have to take the needs of one's twin sibling into consideration.
- When your children talk to you, listen and listen well.
- Be trustworthy.
- Don't. Waste. Time.

1. Laura Markham, "5 Strategies That Prevent Most Misbehavior," *Aha! Parenting,* August 4, 2016, http://www.ahaparenting.com/BlogRetrieve. aspx?PostID=469919&A=SearchResult&SearchID= 10662406&ObjectID=469919&ObjectType=55.

2. Robert Brooks and Sam Goldstein, *Raising Resilient Children: Fostering Strength, Hope, and Optimism in Your Child* (New York: McGraw-Hill, 2002).

3. Stephen Covey, *The 7 Habits of Highly Effective Families* (New York: Golden Books, 1997).

4. Ellen Galinsky, *Ask the Children: What America's Children Really Think about Working Parents* (New York: William Morrow and Company, 1999).

# CHAPTER FIVE

# Value the Singleton

*It's hard to compete with them.*

—Hillary

I magine how it must feel, as a singleton child, to be greeted by your parent's acquaintance with, "Oh, aren't you cute! And what is your name, little one—oh, wait! Are THEY twins?! Identical? Aren't they adorable!" Sooner than you can say your name, the adult has moved swiftly past you to your twin siblings, completely enchanted with them and completely forgetting to finish the greeting with you.

Or how it might feel to walk into a relative's home with your siblings and hear, "The twins are here!"

Singleton siblings must grapple with the feeling of being less exciting than their twin siblings in almost every setting where they are all together. Luke, brother of twins Harriet and Jordan, said he didn't remember feeling inferior to his twin siblings as they grew up together. But recently, after returning home from college for a holiday and watching family videos with his parents, he realized he must have felt that way. "In almost every frame," Luke said, "I was jumping up and down or darting across the room to ensure that I was in front of the camera. Even when my dad was trying to film Harriet or Jordan doing something, there I was, waving my hand or putting my face right in front of the camera. I guess I felt that I needed to be proactive in getting attention."

In addition to feeling hungry for attention, singleton children might also face the realization that they will not have the same relationship with either twin sibling as the twins have with each other. The unique bond twins share means it's often difficult for the non-twin sibling to feel comparatively close to her twin siblings. "They shared the same classes, the same teachers, the same friends, the same hobbies, the same clothes," one singleton interviewee, Hillary, said about her twin sisters. "It was hard to compete with that."

Singleton siblings also can feel out of place in a family where there are only pairs: Mom and Dad, twin and twin. A singleton could wonder, *Where's my partner?* Anton had younger twin brothers and said that his brothers never made him feel left out, but he noticed early on that he didn't have the same bond with either of them as they had with each other. "I felt like the odd man out. My parents had each other. My brothers had each other. And I had the dog."

Anton continued, "I always joked about that, but it just came from the fact that I felt like I didn't have the same connection to someone else in the family that everyone else did."

To confound the issue, twins often use their relationship to gang up on their non-twin sibling, regardless of whether the twins are older or younger than their sibling.

Did you know the Bully Brothers when you were a kid? Those were the siblings who terrorized your block. They hung out at your playground. They threw rocks at their peers and cursed at the young kids. If your twins find power in their relationship and act like the Bully Brothers at home with their non-twin sibling, then there's a strong chance they're acting like the Bully Brothers to those outside the home. You should monitor this behavior and do everything you can to prevent it.

It may, at first, appear to be a fine line between teasing among siblings and bullying. In *The Bullying Antidote: Superpower Your Kids for Life*, Dr. Louise Hart notes, "Normal teasing, which bonds children to each other, is characterized by acceptance, playfulness, and fondness, and it comes and goes. The power balance is usually even."[1] But it crosses over to bullying when one child (or one team of siblings) is consistently asserting mental or physical power over another child.

Dr. Hart suggests that a great way to combat bullying behaviors in one's children is to create a family culture that encourages connection.[2] Commit to relationship-growing routines that include eating dinner together, greeting each other every day with hugs, recalling fun family memories, and celebrating the accomplishments of one another.

Even in cases where the twin siblings don't share a special language, don't spend every waking moment together, and aren't the best of friends, the non-twin sibling still may feel like an outsider simply because she doesn't share the same birthday and commonality of daily experiences.

Should a parent whose first children are twins consider the effect the twins will have on a future child? The following are common questions and issues that arise when parents have twin and singleton children.

# What Impact Does the Non-Twin Sibling Have on The Twins?

Some twin interviewees told me that they felt their parents over-compensated and sometimes spoiled their non-twin siblings. Parents might, for example, give the singleton child a gift on the twins' birthday so that the singleton didn't feel left out, but the parents would not give the twins each a gift on the singleton child's birthday. The parents might allow the singleton child to have two desserts or stay up later than the twins. The parents might allow the singleton to bring a friend along on a family outing so each child had a companion (the assumption being that the twin children would serve as companions to each other). This has multiple un-desired consequences: unfair treatment of the twins, because you're not allowing them to each bring a non–family member friend on the outing; reinforcement of the presumption that the twins are each other's first choice in companionship; and omission of the op-portunity for the singleton child to bond with the twin children.

Twin interviewees reported that when the singleton was given special treatment, the twin children took note and felt resentful. As one individual explained, "*Fair* means *the same* to a child, so when something is done differently for one child, it feels unfair to the others." (The difference between *fair* and *equal* will be discussed at length in Chapter Six). Triplet interviewees Josie, Lisa, and Thomas had an adopted older brother, Len. Each triplet reported that his or her parents seemed to give special treatment to Len to "compen-sate for the fact that he wasn't a triplet and getting all the attention we were otherwise getting." They remembered that he was allowed to misbehave and wouldn't be disciplined. "Our parents felt that he was acting out because he felt isolated, so it wasn't his fault," Josie noted. Thomas remembered his parents bribing Len with a waterbed if he earned an A in a class in which he was struggling.

None of the triplets were offered such a "sweet deal." Lisa recalled that their parents let Len drink soda with dinner when the rest of them were not so permitted. Despite feeling that their parents gave an inordinate amount of special treatment to Len, none of the triplets felt angry at their parents. They felt that their parents were doing the best they could under difficult circumstances. From our discussions, I had the feeling that the triplets, who were all very close with each other, felt a sense of guilt that they were not as close with Len. I think that guilt mitigated any resentment they might have felt toward their parents for giving Len special treatment.

There were also twins who envied the singleton child with respect to her opportunity to go through life solo. A good example of the benefits perceived by twins is the singleton's experience engaging in extracurricular activities. The singleton child was able to partake in activities alone without a family member sidekick. This enabled her to be successful in her own right, to not be compared to another family member, and to have one hundred percent of the attention at games or performances.

The singleton child was also almost always given his own room and didn't have to share with siblings. It was never presumed that the singleton would share his room if logistics required otherwise, but there was a presumption that the twin children would share a room until they expressed a desire not to.

# Does Birth Order Matter?

Radio and television personality Art Linkletter would definitely say that birth order matters. He famously quipped that his "first child with a bloody nose was rushed to the emergency room. The fifth child with a bloody nose was told to go immediately to the yard and stop bleeding on the carpet."

Most parents of multiple children can relate to the change in attitude with each subsequent child, which naturally results from simply gaining experience with the previous children. But shifting from the parent's perspective to the child's, it's important to consider what impact birth order has on the singleton child's ability to feel special. There's a common theory that a child suffers some trauma when her status as the only child is threatened by the arrival of a new baby to the home. A child who previously enjoyed the full attention of parents, grandparents, caregivers, and family friends is now forced to share the limelight with a newer, younger, fresher model—one whose coos, gurgles, and drools curiously appear to fascinate otherwise intelligent-seeming adults. Many sociologists dispute that it's only the older child who suffers from having a sibling. The younger child, too, can feel the fear of displacement when she witnesses a parent's approval and adoration of an older sibling.

Fear of displacement, and the related fear of abandonment, are very real, as any parent who walks faster than her toddler will tell you ("Don't leave me!").

For my non-twin (singleton) interviewees, the ones who were older than their twin siblings generally felt that being older was beneficial. The older singleton sibling has some time to enjoy his parents' undivided attention before the twin siblings come into the family. The younger twins also tend to look up to the older sibling, which makes him feel special.

There were some older singleton children who felt that once the twins came into the family, a gross amount of attention was given to them because they were babies and because there was the "added cuteness factor" of being twins. Some singletons reported that the arrival of twins meant the disruption of what they perceived to be their perfect family grouping of two parents and one child; it interfered with what they had grown to believe was already a complete family unit. This off-setting of status quo and significant change in parent-child ratio caused some behavioral issues in the older singleton child. The singleton child would behave poorly because she needed attention in the face of parents and relatives who were devoting an inordinate amount of attention to the twin newcomers.

When the singleton child is younger than the twins, a different dynamic emerges. The respondents who were younger than their twin siblings generally felt that being younger was beneficial. When the twins left the house after high school, this gave the singleton child a chance to feel like an only child with a large amount of parental attention. Surprisingly, this extra attention was generally welcomed, even for children who were trying to gain independence from their parents in adolescent years.

Still, for some singleton children who have older twin siblings, there was a sense that they were not very close with the twins. In those cases, it appears that the twin siblings had developed a bond for years before the singleton

Notably, twin infants typically bond with *both* parents sooner than singleton infants. In the case of a singleton, the baby bonds sooner and more strongly with the primary caregiver—the one who takes the laboring oar with regard to feedings, diapering, and soothing. For twin infants, the primary caregiver typically needs another caregiver to help out in the early years more frequently than a parent of a singleton would. When that secondary caregiver is the other parent, the twin infants tend to bond with both parents at a much earlier age than their singleton counterparts, who have a significant bond with only the primary caregiving parent.

child was born. So, in addition to the fact that the twins were close by virtue of their twinship, they also had all this extra time to form a bond and create memories together, without the singleton sibling.

Whether older or younger, the singleton child has an opportunity to feel special with the simple use of language. When parents refer to the child as either "the firstborn" or "the youngest," the child is given a reason to feel unique and valued. The mere nomenclature designates that the child holds an important place in the family pecking order. (At the risk of sounding contrary to my own advice, I will share with you that as the youngest of four children, I was referred to as "the baby," which I did not like). Maybe avoid "the baby" and stick to "the youngest" or something of that ilk.

## Does Gender Matter?

The issue of gender often came up when I asked questions about how a singleton child adjusted. Regardless of whether the singleton child was male or female, when the child was a different gender than her twin siblings, she felt special. This, of course, is a dynamic that can only occur when there are same-gender twins and the singleton is of a different gender. This allowed the singleton to be, for instance, "the only daughter," which made her feel unique and valued.

## Should a Parent Proactively Encourage the Twins to Include Their Non-Twin Sibling(s)?

Answers were overwhelmingly similar for this question. Most interviewees felt that their parents should have been more assertive in pushing the twin children to include the singleton child(ren) in play and activities. In fact, this sentiment was expressed by most interviewees, whether a twin or singleton; all felt that the parents should have worked harder to integrate all children in the family and to discourage the twins from bullying the non-twin sibling or doing anything that excluded him.

Samuel is the younger brother of twins Arielle and Ilana. When he was a young child, they would tease him or take his toys. Their parents disciplined Arielle and Ilana when they observed the behavior. As the twins matured, they ceased tormenting Samuel, but he still felt left out because they seemed to have little interest in incorporating him into their activities, especially in middle school. He also felt envious of all the attention they received from family and friends. He was "pretty sour on having twin sisters" until the whole family went to the Twins Day Festival in Twinsburg, Ohio, when Samuel was in eighth grade and Arielle and Ilana were in high school. It was there that he gained an appreciation for how special it was to have twins in the family. He remembered feeling "cool" when his parents bought him a T-shirt that read "Brother of Twins," and he felt a certain camaraderie with others wearing similar "sibling of twins" shirts.

Parents should recognize that singleton children may feel more of a need to find a buddy, a playmate, or a special confidant similar to what they witness their twin siblings having with each other. Many non-twin siblings with whom I talked stated that they were able to form tight bonds with other children and maintain those cherished friendships in their older years. They remarked that they did not observe their twin siblings sharing that same experience of forming close-knit friendships outside the family.

A well-meaning parent will have trouble treating everyone fairly when it comes to family-made decisions, like where to go on vacation or what movie to see or whether to bring a pet into the household. Singleton interviewees reported that voting blocs emerged that would disempower the singleton children. For instance, in families with one singleton child and one set of twins, the parents' interests are aligned, the twins' interests are aligned, and the singleton child must advocate for his own interests. The singleton child's interests, however, represent only one-fifth of the family and thus will be undervalued. But when parents try to deflate the balloon of a voting bloc, they can still do harm. One twin interviewee commented that in her family, she and her twin received one vote (total) for the both of them. She resented that her parents just assumed that she and her sister would vote the same way. The lesson here? A parent cannot win! Each family dynamic is different, so there may be a clear and obvious way to manage the family democracy. The arrangement may need to be fluid, and it may be wise to assess the decision-making process periodically to evaluate whether there's any hurtful disparity in whose voices are being heard.

# What Can Parents Proactively Do to Encourage Healthy Emotional Growth of the Singleton Child?

Parents should consistently emphasize the uniqueness of each child. Each twin should feel unique and special in his own right. Each singleton child should also feel unique and special in his own right. In other words, if a parent is doing her job in ensuring each child feels special, the singleton child will feel just as valued as the twin children—and vice versa!

When others *ooh* and *ahh* over the twins, make sure to alert the person to the specialness of the singleton child. As an example, if you had twins Samantha and Jonathan and singleton Jane, you could say, "Yes, Samantha and Jonathan both are fun; Samantha likes to jump, and Jonathan like to dance. And Jane here is a wonderful helper—she loves to clean the floor when something spills." That way, you are showing your children and the listener that each child is unique in his own way and that you love and value the distinguishing characteristics of each child.

Parents should also, as advised in Chapter Four, schedule alone time with the singleton child. In fact, all of the tips for one-on-one time with your twin children apply for your singleton child(ren) as well. All children deserve special alone time with a parent so they can talk and feel heard. In addition to really listening to one's child, a parent should seek other ways to gain a true understanding of each child. In *The Book of Nurturing: Nine Natural Laws for Enriching Your Family Life*, Linda and Richard Eyre recommend that you "gather intelligence and insight from your child's friends and teachers."[3] This will help you see all of the many facets of their aptitudes, interests, and feelings.

Licensed social worker and mother of twins Tonya McDaniel and her husband Matt have the following dialogue with their singleton child, who is four years older than her twin siblings:

Mom: Who were we before we had you?

Child: Boring Tonya and Matt.

Mom: And who did we become after you were born?

Child: Mommy and Daddy.

This is a beautiful way to pay tribute to the singleton, who may feel less special than her twin siblings. Of course, this works only for older singletons. When the singleton is younger, you could say something like, "We knew we wanted you after we had your twin siblings. That's why we kept trying to become pregnant again—so we could have you in our family."

In order to ensure the emotional health of your singleton child(ren), consider the emotional health of your family as a unit. Is your family close? How can you build a family connection so that each family member feels safe and welcome in the family unit?

# Tips for Bringing Your Family Closer

- Make sure every child in your family knows that your love for him is incomparable. Sibling rivalry and jealousy can often be avoided when each child knows that his parents' love for him is uncontested.
- Make your home a safe place where kids can be themselves without fear of judgment from peers or teachers.
- Encourage frequent expressions of appreciation of everyone in the household. Expressing gratitude toward each family member for a specific action or event should be a weekly, if not daily, activity that your family engages in together. Each child should be taught to regularly verbalize sincere compliments to each sibling (and parent, if I may add!).
- Discourage harmful fighting among your children. Clashes are inevitable and even healthy. They provide an opportunity for your children to learn how to talk through differences and resolve conflicts. Fighting becomes harmful when it is violent or causes

physical injury; that kind of fighting should be quashed immediately.

- Open the lines of communication—ensure that your children feel free to come to you to discuss any issue, whether family-related or not, without fear of overreaction or harsh judgment from you.

- Be together. This becomes harder when your all of your children have different sports games and birthday parties to attend. Find the time during the weekend to have at least one family event in which every family member participates. Maybe it's Friday night dinner, which everyone helps prepare; Saturday night movie-and-popcorn-on-the-couch, where each week, you take turns choosing the movie that everyone will watch; or Sunday evening board-game night, where a prize increases the stakes.

# Tips for Valuing the Singleton Child

- Spend frequent alone time with your singleton child.
- Ensure that the singleton child has plenty of one-on-one time with each twin child, separate from the other one, so that she can bond with each individual member of the twinship.
- While alone time is important, it is equally important to encourage all your children to play with one another and not spend a disproportionate amount of time with only one sibling.
- Acknowledge the singleton child's unique contribution to the family dynamic.
- Don't make the singleton child personally responsible for the care or well-being of her twin siblings.

- When strangers *ooh* and *ahh* over your twin children, make sure to bring the stranger's attention to your singleton child, who also has wonderful features.
- Do not allow your twin children to bully or team up against the singleton child.
- Employ language such as "our only daughter," "first-born," or "youngest" to highlight that your singleton child holds a special place in the family.
- Try to avoid democratic family processes (no matter how well intended) that end up undervaluing any one child's interests.
- While you want your singleton child to feel special, do not overemphasize the specialness or engage in what would be perceived by your twin children as unfair special treatment.
- Bring your family closer with an atmosphere of playfulness, abundant expressions of unconditional love and gratitude, a judgment-free home, intolerance for violent behavior, and open lines of communication.

1. Louise Hart, *The Bullying Antidote: Superpower Your Kids for Life*, (Center City, MN: Hazelden, 2013), 65.

2. Ibid, 65–6, 158–9.

3. Linda and Richard Eyre, *The Book of Nurturing: Nine Natural Laws for Enriching Your Family Life* (New York: McGraw-Hill, 2003).

# CHAPTER SIX

# Don't Compare

There can only be one first-chair violin.

—Jeannie

Comparisons are inevitable. Labeling is inevitable. Competition is inevitable. This is because you cannot raise your twin children in a vacuum without exposure to the outside world. You cannot always control what others say to your children. And you can almost never control how your children will internalize what they hear. This chapter is designed to help you mitigate the effects of the inevitable.

# Comparisons, Labeling, and Competition

From the day they were born (literally), people were comparing and labeling my twin daughters. Because of their nursing behaviors, the maternity ward nurses called Tal "the Troublemaker" and Eden "the Easy One." At first, Tal didn't latch very well to my breast and kept falling asleep. Of course, were she the only baby at my breast, the nurse would likely chalk this behavior up to being— oh, I don't know—a baby. But because *in comparison to Eden* Tal wasn't feeding as efficiently, she was called The Troublemaker. Looked at separately, neither infant had any peculiar idiosyncrasies—each performed as any hungry newborn should. But looked at in comparison to one another, Tal seemed deficient. The maternity nurses, and many adults after them, sought to apply labels immediately. This propensity for labeling seemed to be connected to the adults' need to figure out how to distinguish one child from the other.

As my daughters aged, the number of labels increased. The Bruiser, the Dancer, the Sleeper, the Talker, the Crier, the Helper, the Sweet One, the Hyper One, the Verbal One, the Artistic One. At times, labels would migrate from one daughter to the other, depending on which child was exhibiting which behavior in front of which adult. One thing was clear: those who were so quick to label my children didn't really *know* my children. Sure, labeling my two-year-old daughter "the Athletic One" made sense the day she threw the tennis ball with better facility than children twice her age. But my other daughter that same week showed impressive aptitude when climbing a ladder at the playground. Neither child's physical achievement was so remarkable that it eclipsed the achievement of her sister. Yet by labeling one daughter "the athletic one," the unspoken suggestion is that the other daughter was non-athletic. A more proper use of language would have been to call the mobile child simply "athletic." This adjective enables the adult to express his observation about the child without indirectly labeling the child's sister.

Imagine fourteen-year-old twins hearing a parent's friend comment, "Ohhhh . . . so he's the Academic One." The twin adolescent who was not labeled "academic" hears that he is perceived to be not academic. What does that make him then? What is the opposite of being academic? Does it make him "not smart" or "less smart" by default? *What's the point in trying to get better grades?* he might wonder. *This is how people perceive me—it must be true. My brother is the Academic One, the Smart One. I am the non-academic one, the dumb one.* Thus, not only do labels represent people's ill-conceived perceptions, they have the dangerous consequence of leading to self-fulfilling prophecies.

Of course, parents who don't have twin children will tell you that labeling happens in every family, for children who are not necessarily twins. This phenomenon is present in any family dynamic where adults want to show that they're recognizing certain personality traits, hobbies, interests, or talents that are unique to a child in comparison to the other children in the family. This is absolutely true—children who are in a family with other children tend to be labeled in one way or another. For them, these labels could become self-fulfilling prophecies as well.

The difference with twins is that the comparisons start from the very beginning and are more apples-to-apples than apples-to-oranges. A direct comparison with a peer who is the same age and undergoing most of the same experiences in life is certainly more impactful than a comparison with siblings who are older or younger. Twin interviewees reported to me that comparisons made them feel angry or resentful not only toward the person who compared them but also toward their co-twin, to whom they were being compared.

For example, twin interviewee Jeannie and her identical sister, Evelyn, were from a "traditional Korean family," which Jeannie described as "the kind where the parents pressured their children to be excellent in both school and music." The parents enrolled them in the same music program as children, and Evelyn showed early and impressive talent at the violin. Jeannie was a very good violinist as well, but "there can only be one first-chair violinist," and that was Evelyn. That Jeannie wasn't the better musician meant that Jeannie had to excel in her parents' other valued category: education. Jeannie was one of the top five students in her graduating high school class. From a distance, the strong motivation to excel might appear to parents to be a wonderful trait to have your children display; it might even seem like the result of top-notch parenting.

From the inside, however, the drive to perfection, fueled by competition with one's twin sibling, was detrimental to the twin relationship. Jeannie and Evelyn started out as "buddies" and enjoyed having each other as playmates in kindergarten and the early years of elementary school. They would follow each other around on the playground, make up secret handshakes, and build forts in their basement on cold winter days. But once school shifted from emphasizing skill-building to emphasizing academics, things started to change. Their parents would constantly compare the twins to each other and say things like, "Your *identical* twin sister received a perfect score on this exam—why didn't you?" Jeannie and Evelyn would often be the top two contenders in their science team's invention contest or the school's spelling bee. When music was offered as an option, the parents urged them both to play the violin, even though Jeannie would have preferred to play a different instrument and, later, no instrument at all. After the introduction of the violin, Jeannie felt that, whether she chose to be or not, she was stuck in a never-ending cutthroat contest with Evelyn. Memories of their close friendship faded with age, and they grew into fierce rivals. Jeannie recalls being put on a team project where she, Evelyn, and one other student were on the same team. When the other student came to their house, Jeannie recalls with embarrassment that she and Evelyn fought the whole time in front of the other student.

When their parents applied more pressure for perfection, Jeannie and Evelyn would address their parents' criticisms with attacks on one another. Fights with their parents often escalated to door slams following screams of "Just because I'm not perfect at physics like Jeannie, the poster child!" and "Evelyn is first-chair because she kisses the conductor's butt!" Jeannie was unable to remember a time since middle school when she did not feel acrimonious toward Evelyn.

They attended the same college because they both really wanted to attend this particular school, but they lived in different dorms, pursued different majors, and spent time in different social groups. That separation helped them move beyond their mutual disdain. Now, both graduate students and living in different cities, they talk on the phone every one to two months. Their relationship is civil but strained.

In looking back, Jeannie surmises that it was the competition between her and Evelyn that started the unraveling of the tight bond they enjoyed as children. She believes her parents fueled the competition by forcing them into the same activities and by emphasizing that each child had to be the best at every endeavor. Obviously, it's impossible for each child to be the best at the exact same activity at the exact same time. These unrealistic expectations, coupled with the failure to allow each child to pursue her own interests, reveal that the appearance of stellar parenting can often betray reality.

A German study from 1934 that modern scientists rely on reveals that Jeannie's and Evelyn's cutthroat attitudes toward each other is the exception rather than the rule. Helmut von Bracken observed young identical twins and young fraternal twins who were asked to complete different tasks, such as solving math problems. The identical twins worked together to achieve what they perceived to be a joint goal, while the fraternal twins became rivals, trying to outscore one another. Scientists concluded that identical twins are more inclined than fraternal twins to cooperate with one another.[1] This was corroborated by my interview with Justin, who said of his twin, "We were never competitive against each other, just against everyone else. I never cared if he was number one and I was number two—so long as we were both at the top."

But the majority of twins I interviewed did feel competitive against their twin, and they had negative memories related to it. Lacey's father was always pitting her against her twin. If they would be running in the backyard, their father would yell, "Beat her! You can do it!" She always understood this to be a way to motivate her to do better, but, in retrospect, she says that it made her feel like she was always in a battle with her sister. "I remember being in a math class and there was a girl there who was jealous that I got a higher score than she did on a test. For the next test, I purposely made mistakes so she would get a higher grade than I did. I would have never done that with my sister. With my sister, I just wanted to beat her and win. But I was not competitive like that with anyone else."

Monozygotic twins are generally compared to each other more often than dizygotic twins. For female identical twins whose bodies took different forms and shapes as they grew, there was the added complication of one twin being heavier than the other. The more fit twin would feel guilty about her looks as the heavier twin felt unattractive in comparison to her twin sibling. One interviewee described looking at her twin as seeing her mirror image, but not a perfect replica of herself; instead she saw the idealized image, with the body she had always wanted but struggled (and failed) to ever achieve.

Identical twins have told me they felt "hardwired" to compare themselves to each other because people were constantly trying to find ways to distinguish them from their twin siblings. This hardwiring also resulted in these individuals constantly comparing themselves to their peers. *I'm better at math. My paper is not as well-written as his. My thesis is more relevant.* "It took a lot of self-awareness to realize that the rest of the world didn't operate that way, with constant scorekeeping," one interviewee said. "The only one who really cared how I fared against my peers at graduate school was me."

But regardless of zygosity, twins, by virtue of their concordant ages, will be compared to each other. And when they are, it's hard for them not to feel inadequate at some point. *My twin sibling is really good at basketball, and I'm not. Something must be wrong with me,* a twin might think. Parents and others obviously can fuel this erroneous thought pattern by making observational comparisons, no matter how innocently intended. A teacher's passing comment—"Wow, Jaimee is a really talented writer"—can inadvertently make Jaimee's twin feel like an inadequate writer.

To counterbalance comparisons iterated by others in their children's life, parents can proactively guide their children in managing comparisons. They can encourage good self-esteem by focusing on the unique talents each child possesses that have import in and of themselves, regardless of who else possesses those talents. One twin interviewee mentioned fondly that her mother used to say to her, "Compare yourself to yourself, not to your twin brother or anyone else." Another twin interviewee appreciated it when his parents said, "Look, we're proud of you both. Just because Jessica got a couple of points higher on the SAT doesn't take away from the fact that you did great on the SAT as well. You both studied hard, and it shows. We're really proud of both of you."

To further avoid intra-twin comparisons, and to encourage the distinct talents and interests of each child, a parent may wish to enroll the children in different extracurricular classes, allowing each child to shine on his own. Of course, this is much easier to advise than to implement. Different classes means more coordinating, possibly more expense (you lose out on the "sibling discount" many vendors offer), and more scheduling of drop-offs and pick-ups. Catering to the individual needs of your individual children will definitely not be more convenient, but the long-term payoff for all parties involved will most likely be worth it.

Parents should rethink their words when they're tempted to call one child "the Helper" or "the Neat One." For the child who is not labeled these things, he might simply assume the role of "the Lazy One" or "the Mess-Maker." No one benefits from those comparisons—as twins age, one twin might be called the "Pretty One" or "the Strong One," which means the other twin will feel like "the Ugly One" or "the Weak One." Keep in mind that you will likely have to coach other adults to respect your rules.

A twin may be told by a parent or teacher, "Your sister Sally got an A in this subject; why didn't you?" I once heard my well-meaning caretaker say to my one-year-old daughter, "Your sister likes the pasta your mommy made. Look how well she's eating it. Why aren't *you* eating the pasta?" But what another child is eating or not eating at the table is of no consequence to the subject. If she doesn't like pasta—or doesn't want pasta at that moment—it should not matter that another individual who happens to be the same age does like pasta. Is there any logical correlation between one child's penchant for a certain food and that of another child? While the caretaker meant well and was only trying to encourage the child to eat (and caretakers of twin toddlers can attest to the frustration of picky eating!), the child may have thought, *I hear you: my sister likes pasta. So what? I don't. Why is that so hard to understand? Please serve me something else already!*

Many twin interviewees told me that while they felt internally competitive with their twin sibling, they never wanted to see their co-twin fail. They tended to praise the success of their co-twins and noted that if they were ever in a competition along with their twin—sports, chess, the spelling bee—their first preference was to win, but if they were to lose, they would rather lose to their twin sibling than to anyone else.

Twin interviewees Shandra and Jackie both applied to the residential governor's school program, a prestigious summer program for academically advanced high school students. "The envelopes came in the mail on the same day," Shandra recalled. "The one with my name on it was thick and Jackie's was thin. We knew before opening that I was accepted and Jackie was not. Jackie was devastated." Shandra felt immensely guilty and, for a moment, even considered not attending the program because she felt sorry for her sister. She felt that she could not enjoy the program knowing how upset Jackie was about not having been accepted.

But when I spoke with Jackie (I interviewed them separately), she described the event differently. She explained that while she was really disappointed that she wasn't accepted into the program, she felt happy for Shandra. She said:

Everything was very awkward. No one, including Shandra, wanted to talk about governor's school around me. Everyone was hypersensitive about it around me, which made it harder for me to move on from it. I think people felt that I couldn't possibly feel happy about Shandra's gain while at the same time feeling sad about my loss, but that's really how I felt. I was sad, but I was also really proud of her.

In addition to competition in school and activities, twins learn early on that they must compete for parental attention. Unlike their singleton counterparts, each child receives less than one hundred percent of the attention a parent gives a child. The twins will share attention, and one twin may receive more than the other, if the parent perceives that child as more needy. Over time, one twin may start to resent the unequal distribution of resources. The child might crave more attention and thus learn to compete for it. That may manifest in more fussy behavior for toddlers and more defiance or regression for older kids.

What can parents do to help mitigate the negative effects of competition between twins? After all, some amount of competition is healthy. There's nothing wrong with a child being

> I enjoyed this story from twins Harry and Greg. When they were home for their respective universities' holiday breaks, they slept in their childhood bedroom, which they shared until they left for college. Their mother was in their room, talking with them before bed. After she said goodnight, she kissed Greg and then Harry. As she was walking out the door, they teased her about how she always kissed Greg first before Harry. She then insisted that when they were younger, she would kiss Harry first and, at some point, she changed it up to appear more fair. "She was so upset about it," laughed Greg. "We totally didn't care—we were just joking! But she was so concerned that Harry really felt hurt about not getting the first kiss!"

motivated to achieve based on the barometers set by peers. It's important, though, for parents to praise both children and focus less on the result and more on the process.

Research on academic and social performance in kids demonstrates that it's more effective to praise a child's efforts, or the process, rather than assign a label to the child. For example, imagine a young child succeeded in putting together an age-advanced puzzle. Rather than saying "Wow! You're so smart!" a parent should say "Wow! You finished the puzzle! Your patience and hard work really paid off!"

Studies have shown that children who are praised for their ability ("You're so smart!") tend to view any failure, no matter how nominal, as evidence of a lack of that ability (the child thinks *I must be dumb*). These children tend to completely give up or perform more poorly after a failure, or they seek less challenging tasks so as to avoid any possibility of failure. They also show inordinate concern for how they measure up against their peers. Children who are praised for their effort ("You worked really hard on that!"), on the other hand, show minimal or no concern for how they measure up against others, demonstrate higher motivation for accomplishing tasks, and seek more difficult challenges.

To help minimize the amount of intra-twin competition, then, a parent should be wary of the words he uses when praising his twin children. Praising the effort or the process and not the ability or quality will help reduce the children's own interest in comparing themselves to each other.

You may notice that one of your twin children lacks self-esteem; this loss of sense of self is common when one twin has a so-called stronger personality. In some cases, one twin will represent both twins—she will speak on the other's behalf, and she will take charge of their activities. It's imperative as a parent to nurture the quieter child and to make her feel special and important.

A parent may also try to encourage her to make decisions for herself and not allow her twin to do so at all times. A parent can give a child a voice by asking questions, showing interest in her special qualities, and giving genuine consideration to her unique wants and desires that differ from that of her twin.

## Who Came First?

Some parents of twins will refuse to tell their children which one was born first. They feel that telling them birth order would somehow create unhealthy competition between them. They are concerned that the information will give the older child an unfair edge and leave the younger twin with a constant feeling of being in the older one's shadow. They don't want any unfounded stereotypes, for instance, that a firstborn twin is more dominant, to influence their children's behaviors. Many adult twins who do not know their birth order seem satisfied with their parents' decision to not disclose the information. They enjoy disappointing people who inquire as to who was the firstborn with shoulder shrugs and honest answers of "I don't know." Their parents taught them that the information has no value or importance, so they simply don't care to know. Obviously, at a certain point, adult twins could learn the information if they wanted to—birth certificates and hospital records would be an easy place to start.

Many of the twins I interviewed, however, were told their birth order, and neither twin expressed a sense of superiority or inferiority because of it. They generally felt that knowing the birth order enabled them to feel more like individuals who had unique birth times and circumstances. Each twin could assume an identity in the family dynamic: oldest, middle, or youngest.

Many people have asked me in front of my children, "Who is older?" And I have always answered honestly. I try to make sure each child feels special. I call Eden my "firstborn" and Tal "my baby" or "my youngest." I certainly didn't see anything wrong with this: I was highlighting their uniqueness and their special-ness. But one day, when four-year old Tal had burst into tears because Eden had learned to swim from one side of the pool to the other, she cried, "Look at what Eden can do! And she came out of your belly first and I didn't!"

There are situations that even a well-meaning parent simply cannot master!

# Household Discipline

*Discipline* is an important word to define here. When I refer to it, I do not mean *punish*, as in causing someone to suffer as a means of retribution for certain behavior. When I use the word disci-pline, I refer to teaching, educating, enlightening, training, and coaching. Punishment disempowers children; discipline empow-ers children.

Discipline is an art and a skill. When your child misbehaves, it helps to think of the episode as an opportunity to educate your child on how to do it differently the next time (and, at least in the case of my kids, the time after that, and the time after that). In most instances, your kid doesn't know better, so you have to teach her. In some instances, your kid does know better and makes a lousy choice. As an adult who is not perfect (forgive me for the real talk here), you probably can relate to making a dumb decision. In thinking back to some of my activities as a teenager, I feel thankful that, despite my stupidity, I was miraculously shielded from what could otherwise have been a disaster. Your children will make bad decisions because children are human. It is how you talk about those decisions with your children that will determine whether you have disciplined or punished them.

The moments after a child makes a bad decision are key because those are what many in the parenting industry call "teaching moments." Whether your kid is an out-of-control toddler or a misguided teen, helping her reflect on her actions will give her the tools she needs to become a well-behaving, good-decision-making grown-up in the real world. Mister Rogers said it best: "I think of discipline as the continual everyday process of helping a child learn self-discipline."

Parents of twins often encounter stumbling blocks when navigating household discipline. When one twin child misbehaves, many parents find it easier to just discipline both children rather than brainstorming a fair way to manage the situation. Many twin interviewees recalled a time when both twins were punished for the wrongdoing of one twin. Parents often used a guilt-by-association model. For instance, when Joey was playing in the living room and knocked over and shattered a precious vase, the parent punished both him and his twin sister, Terri, by sending them to their rooms, even though Terri hadn't touched the vase.

When twin siblings are almost always together, it seems to make sense for parents to assume that one twin was the willing accomplice of the other. Often, one twin is the wrongdoer and the other twin, while not actively engaging in the undesirable behavior, does not try to prevent their co-twin from doing it. Whether a parent should discipline the twin who stood idly by depends on the parent's philosophy on personal accountability and responsibility in the presence of a peer's wrongdoing.

What about disciplining twin children for fighting with one another? Studies of siblings reveal that, on average, siblings have conflicts with one another nearly five times every day. I imagine, but do not have data, that twins' conflicts carry a higher figure. While parents might fear that these conflicts are destroying the bond between their children, they should instead look at the fights from a different perspective. In many instances, twin children fighting is in part due to their need for parental attention. Professor of evolutionary biology Rebecca Kilner and colleagues authored a study about the competition among cowbird nestlings for food. When the nestlings openly fought with one another, the parents worked harder to bring them food. In fact, displaying competition ensured that the parents would bring more food than if only one chick was demanding to be fed. Paradoxically, the young birds were cooperating by fighting more openly, all for the goal of attaining more parental attention, which led to more food.[2]

Next time your children are fighting with one another in your presence, ask yourself whether what they need is not less of each other but more of you.

Scientific studies have established that humans have a strong inclination toward, and preference for, fairness. In one study led by neuroscientist Tania Singer, participants played a game where some individuals played fairly and some played unfairly. Later, while in an MRI scanner, participants watched as each partner—both fair and unfair—received what appeared to be painful stimuli. When witnessing the fair partners appearing to be in pain, the participants' brain scans showed increased activity in regions demonstrating a high empathic response. But when witnessing the unfair partners appearing to be in pain, participants' brain activities showed increased activity in the reward center, indicating that participants felt satisfied with an establishment of justice through punishment of the previous unfair behavior. In other words, we are wired to favor fairness—and to disfavor unfairness.[3]

# Fair Is Not Always Equal

In attempts to make sure that their twin children don't feel competitive with one another, parents will often treat both children equally, even when ideals of fairness dictate otherwise. A parent may want to "keep the peace" between the twin children and thus give them equal rewards or equal punishment, even when circumstances suggest that the children should be treated differently from one another.

Dr. Terri Apter notes that children in the same family want nothing more than to be seen as unique and different from one another. She explains that "[w]hen grown-ups try to fix things so that they are 'fair,' or so that 'each has the same,' they inevitably fail" because "[e]ach sibling wants to be different, not the same; each wants to be special, not equal."[4]

Besides, being fair does not mean treating your children equally. And treating your children the same is not necessarily fair. An example of treating the children equally is giving them each fifteen dollars at the end of the week for helping around the house. But what if the chores were different or the performance of the chores varied by child? What if one child whose job was to set the table for dinner did so every night of the week and the other child whose job was to clear the table after dinner did so only two nights of the week? In that scenario, fifteen dollars at the end of the week for each child is equal payment but not fair payment. The lesson learned by both children is that their effort, their motivation, and the completion of the task are not related to the compensation for it. Children may also falsely gather that they will always be treated equally by parents and others regardless of their actions and behaviors.

Your twin children are different individuals with different (mis)behaviors, different learning styles, and different needs at different times. Treating them the same not only reinforces the misconception that they are not separate, unique individuals but also prevents you from addressing the individual needs of the child. Treating your children the same means you don't see their actions or needs as distinct from one another.

Treating your children fairly means giving your children what they need to be successful. It can be tricky for parents of twins to overcome the temptation to do things equally when what's equal is not what's fair. It's hard to explain why your children received different punishments, consequences, or other discipline. And worse, it's hard for the children to understand. But even though the concepts of not-equal-but-fair are high level, parents should do their best to clearly and frequently explain the motivations for these carefully conceived household disciplinary rules. It may be helpful to explain that you think of each child as unique. You may also encourage the child to imagine she was a singleton in the same situation; she would naturally receive a consequence that relates directly to her action without relation to another individual's separate and distinct action and consequence.

## About Envy

My grandmother, Sara Mayers, discouraged the use of the word *jealous*; she felt we should use the word *admire* instead. At first, I understood her preference as one designed to protect the speaker from sounding spiteful and unkind, as though by stating that I was jealous of someone, I risked being negatively perceived by others. I felt grateful for the lesson. I did feel that by saying that I *admired* someone else, I sounded far less catty than saying that I was *jealous* of her.

I later learned that Grandma Sara's protest of the word *jealous* had very little to do with others' perceptions and was actually a tool she used for her own peace of mind and heart. Whenever she began to feel envious of another, she reminded herself that it was neither productive nor healthy to covet what someone else had. Rather than wanting what the other person had and emphasizing what she lacked, she was better off simply reframing the feeling as admiration. To admire was Grandma Sara's way of being both gracious and self-healing.

Thus, it is not without a twinge of guilt that I write about what I consider to be an inevitable part of twin sibling relationships: jealousy. Envy is not simply reduced to wanting what someone else has. In fact, psychologists have discovered that envy is the sensation we feel when we recognize that what the other person has in some way diminishes who we ourselves are. In the context of siblings being envious of one another, the jealousy is often rooted in a fear that a sibling's good qualities will in some way deprive the other sibling of love—from their parents, relatives, caregivers, teachers, and friends.

Dr. Apter explains that studies of envy among siblings reveal that the more similar the siblings are, the more likely they are to feel jealous of one another. "It has often been observed," she writes, "that envy is not sharpest when the discrepancy between oneself and another is greatest, but when we are up close, standing side by side, measuring small differences in a context of broad similarities." In other words, it is the "similar status and common background and shared personal connections that make a sibling threatening."[5] For twins, then, whose backgrounds, histories, and personal connections could not be more similar, the potential for jealousy is that much greater.

Envy is inevitable, but parents might find it fruitful to take a page from Grandma Sara's playbook: reframe envy as admiration. Encourage your children to recognize and celebrate the greatness of one another. Genuine expressions of fondness, appreciation, and praise can be contagious—and good cheer among children is definitely worth spreading.

# Tips for Avoiding Comparisons, Competition, and Labeling

- Recognize that twins never really have a break from having another peer around with whom they compete, disagree, fight, and compare against.
- Remind yourself that your twin children, while the same age, are different and unique. They have different tastes and passions—different appetites, different food preferences, and different musical interests.
- Avoid comparisons between your twin children.
- Never refer to a child as "the _____ One," whether in the presence of the child or not.
- When others label your children in your presence, immediately use language to counter the putative harm that may have been done. Explain that neither child is "the _____ One," as they both have such-and-such attributes.
- Help caretakers develop their view of your twins as individuals in their own respective rights.
- Coach caretakers on what language to use and what language to avoid in front of your twin children.
- If you hear a caretaker inadvertently compare the children, kindly point out the error and suggest different ways of communicating in those moments.
- Try to understand early on the unique interests of each child, and enroll your children in separate enrichment programs or classes accordingly.

- Praise your children's effort, or the process, rather than their ability.
- If one child shows submissive qualities in relation to the more outgoing behavior of the other, encourage the quieter twin to express her needs and desires and make sure her voice is being heard.
- Remember that equal is not necessarily fair and fair is not necessarily equal. There will be times when parents will have to treat their twin children unequally because, by doing so, the parent is treating the children fairly.

1. Helmut von Bracken, "Mutual Intimacy in Twins: Types of Social Structure in Pairs of Identical and Fraternal Twins," *Journal of Personality* 2, no. 4 (1934): 293–309, doi: 10.1111/j.1467-6494.1934.tb02106.x.

2. Rebecca Kilner, Joah R. Madden, and Mark E. Hauber, "Brood Parasitic Cowbird Nestlings Use Host Young to Procure Resources," *Science* 305, no. 5685 (2004): 877–9, http://science.sciencemag.org/content/305/5685/877.

3. Tania Singer et al., "Empathic Neural Responses Are Modulated by the Perceived Fairness of Others," *Nature* 439, no. 7075 (2006): 466–9, https://www.ncbi.nlm.nih.gov/pmc/articles/PMC2636868/pdf/ukmss-3669.pdf.

4. Apter, *The Sister Knot*.

5. Ibid.

# CHAPTER SEVEN

# School: To Separate or Not to Separate

Teachers confused us; teachers compared us.

—Florence

Administrators and teachers generally agree that separation of twin siblings is good for the children academically, emotionally, and socially. While having a twin sibling present could ease first-day nerves and provide a general safe haven for a child, this built-in comfort could actually impede the child's emotional growth and courage-building. From my interviews with educators and twins (and some parents), it became clear that there are a host of factors to consider when determining whether and when to separate your children in school. Let's look at these factors from the viewpoints of the different actors at play.

# Educators

Of all the school administrators I interviewed, there were very few who felt that twins should generally be kept together. A child is given the chance to be an individual with unique characteristics in the classroom setting and is able to grow from the opportunity to be individualized by authority figures and peers. And separation helps prevent teachers from confusing one twin for the other, especially in cases of identical twins.

Separation also helped mitigate the dreaded comparisons between the twins. Teachers who have twin children in the same classroom often compare them to each other. Twins' class participation, homework quality, and exam scores are barometers for measuring each child's success in comparison to the other. Some teachers admitted to me that they had to bite their tongue because the temptation was so strong to say something like, "Ben completed the homework assignment. Why didn't you?"

All the school administrators I interviewed unanimously agreed that teachers should not compare twin children to each other and should recognize that each child is an individual with different needs, abilities, and interests. Yet many of them admitted to comparing the children behind closed doors. In many a teachers' lounge across the country, teachers discuss twin students with each other. Two teachers who have one twin each will compare notes about how each child behaves and remark on the similarities and differences. These teachers do not make these comparisons maliciously. The conversations are generally motivated by a desire to find the best resolution to issues and challenges faced by the twin students.

For those educators who did think twins should be kept together, they noted that the more extroverted twin could help the introverted twin feel comfortable. They thought that the built-in support that twins have is more beneficial than harmful. With regard to learning, children who were in the same class could study together. For example, with a foreign language, twins who were in the same class were able to practice oral proficiency and engage in foreign language dialogues at home. The teachers also saw that it was easier on parents when twins were kept together because parents didn't have to keep track of different teachers, homework assignments, and curricula. They also noted that keeping the twins together in school ensured equality of educational opportunity and experience. There is no conclusive data as to whether twins placed together in every grade performed academically better or worse in school than twins who were separated. There have been smaller-scale studies that show that twins perform better than non-twins on joint problem-solving tasks, with monozygotic twins performing even better than dizygotic twins.

Many administrators complained to me that in discussing whether to separate their twin children, many parents resisted the notion that separation would be beneficial for their children. It seemed to be a natural instinct for parents to want to keep their children together, and it was challenging for the administrators to convince these parents that separation was a positive thing and would likely be in the best interests of the children.

## Twins

The twins I interviewed tended to generally agree that separation from their twin sibling in school was a good thing. Some opined that the reason they had a close relationship with each other throughout childhood and adulthood was because of the separation in school. The separation enabled them a structured space in which to be themselves and grow independently from the other. And at the end of the day, the twins could reconvene and compare notes on what they each experienced in their respective unique environments. They could share funny stories about their teachers, discuss the books they were reading, or complain about their homework assignments.

Twin interviewees Selma and Dahlia were in separate classes but in the same school from first grade through eighth grade. They attended different high schools because Selma, who excelled in science and math, was accepted into a special science and technology high school. Selma noted that the separation was great for their relationship. It helped reduce competition-fueled fights. She also remarked, "My new friends didn't learn I was a twin until they came to the house. That was cool too."

Triplets Devon, Patricia, and Alecia tended to be competitive with each other, whether socially or academically. To alleviate some of the competition and help each child find their individuality, their mother sought different classes for them. In the large public school system in which they were enrolled, this was possible even at the kindergarten level. The school district accommodated their mother's request to have each child in a separate kindergarten class, even when that meant sending at least one of the children to a different school within the district.

Some twin interviewees reported that their parents were adamant about separating their twin children. Twin interviewee Justin recalled that from first grade all the way to twelfth grade, he and his twin sister were in separate classes. In middle school, when students were placed in specific academic tracks, Justin and his sister were very similar in their skill sets and academic levels. He recalled that every spring, his mother would go to the guidance counselor's office to help the counselor "figure out this complicated matrix of class schedules for the following year to ensure that my sister and I would never be in the same class." In retrospect, Justin appreciated his mother's tireless efforts to ensure that he and his sister would be in separate classes despite their academic similarities.

On the other hand, there were some twin interviewees who were in separate classes but would have preferred to stay together. One twin felt concerned for his sister when they were separated because his sister had a severe food allergy. By not being with her, he could not warn teachers about his sister's allergy. He recalls feeling constantly worried that his sister would have an anaphylactic attack that he could have otherwise prevented. Another person mentioned that she would have wanted to protect her sister from a peer who was very controlling and had a history of bullying other kids.

Twin interviewee Kyle remembered being in preschool when the teachers tried to separate him and his twin sister, Frannie. It wasn't a permanent class separation; the teacher simply wanted to take Kyle to the music class while Frannie would stay in the arts and crafts room. Kyle remembers crying hysterically while walking down the hallway and being inconsolable until the teacher brought him back to the room where Frannie was calmly coloring on a paper plate. While he acknowledged that Frannie seemed totally unfazed by the separation, Kyle believed they weren't ready to be separated and that the separation, albeit brief, should not have been forced on them.

While the above examples highlight that some twin interviewees thought favorably about keeping twins in the same classroom, these instances also tend to demonstrate the very reason twins should probably be separated as a general rule: an individual needs to learn to be independent and stand on her own. Twins should not be their siblings' keepers. Both emotional and physical codependency between twins are generally seen as unhealthy for each individual's emotional growth.

Where twins are in the same class, group projects present a wonderful opportunity to give them the respective space they need for social and academic growth. A group project is a chance for each twin to participate in a different group to see how they do in a group without their twin affecting behavior, leadership, and learning. An overwhelming majority of the twins I interviewed, however, recounted that when they were in the same class as their twin, teachers tended to place them in the same group. The twins thus missed out on the rare and essential opportunity to develop outside of the presence of the other.

For some triplets in smaller districts where accommodation of separate classrooms was not possible for all three children, some parents choose to alternate which of the triplets stay together every other year. In other words, in first grade, triplet A and B are in the same class while triplet C is in a different class. In second grade, B and C are in the same class while A is in a different class. In third grade, A and C are in the same class while B is in a different class, and so on.

## Parents

Parents may want to consider that separation may help alleviate potential friction between their twins. Twins are already accustomed to feeling competitive with one another. Being in the same classroom, taking the same exams, and engaging in the same projects present more contexts for them to compete with one another. In most contests, there is only room for one winner, so jealousy and resentment are likely yields from classroom competition.

Additionally, parents may find it even more difficult to refrain from comparing their twins when they are in the same classroom. When their children are in the same class at school, there is even more opportunity to hold one child up to the other's standards in all areas. In fact, many teachers complained that during parent-teacher conferences, which are designed to focus on one child at a time, parents would typically want to discuss the other child as a point of comparison. Teachers often had to redirect the parent ("Yes, Jessica is good at math, but we're talking about Karen now."). Thus, separation in school helps temper the opportunities for comparison between the two children.

Mandatory school policies are also a hot topic among twin parents. The vast majority of twin parents are in favor of policies that do not force separation but instead allow the parents to have meaningful input into the placement of their children. As of the writing of this book, more than a dozen states have laws that mandate parental input into placement decisions, and many more either have sponsored bills or resolutions in favor thereof. In states where there are no such laws or guidelines, a school may legally implement a mandatory separation policy.

There is no one-size-fits-all solution to the issue of whether to separate twins in the school setting. There are a host of factors that are beyond one's control, such as school district policy, availability of different teachers and classrooms for the same age group, and learning differences between siblings. But in the cases where a parent is given the choice as to whether to separate their children, there are several factors to consider.

## Age

In the preschool years, having a twin sibling eased the transition from being at home all day to being in a school setting. There are many "firsts" during this time of a child's life (e.g., first babysitter experience, first playdate, first time at a crowded public outing), and generally those first moments are shared moments. In the pre-school years, there is no main emphasis on academics; the focus is on social and emotional growth. Usually by age three or four, a child is able to express himself clearly, act more independently, and behave less narcissistically. Before that, a lot of social interaction is parallel play and not very interactive.

Preschool administrators tend to agree that keeping twins together at this time is not necessarily harmful unless there is a dominant dynamic between the twins. The dominance is typically manifested in one twin talking on behalf of his sibling. In these cases, the quiet twin sometimes doesn't feel the need to speak because her brother is doing it for her. As a result, her speech may be delayed, as might other elements in her development. In these cases, it is best for the twins to be separated so the quieter child can feel the same sense of urgency for communication that her peers feel and thus learn to communicate at the same pace as her peers. And the dominant twin can focus more on his own needs without the burden of communicating on his sibling's behalf.

A fun test for a parent could be to observe what happens when your preschool-age twin children walk into a classroom separately. Does the child know where to go? Does the child go directly to a toy across the room or to greet another child? Or does the child stand at the door and look for her twin sibling? Hesitation to act without the presence of one's twin is a sign that separation might help a child learn to steer her own ship.

There are other ways of doing this same test. When my twin daughters were toddlers, I would take them to a community play room. The moment we took off our shoes (as required by the establishment), Tal would run off to play with the other kids. Eden would ask to be held as we walked into the play area. After five to ten minutes of observing the room and the kids in it, Eden would allow me to put her down, but she would stay near me and try to engage me in her play. I purposely would stay in one spot to see if Eden would grow bored and move to a different area on her own. Eventually, when she wanted to play across the room, she would look around and ask for Tal. She would see Tal was across the room, running around with much taller and older kids. Eden would run over to that side of the room, calling Tal's name over and over until Tal turned around to acknowledge Eden. I knew that if Tal hadn't been on that side of the room, Eden would not have run over there. It was typically the case that Eden would not engage with other children until she could see Tal engaging with them to no apparent danger. With increased opportunities to be with other kids on her own, Eden was able to develop a greater comfort in playing with them.

Separation will not necessarily change your child's personality from introvert to extrovert, but it will help him lean in to new experiences and develop his own presence in various contexts.

Many administrators I interviewed said that parents tend to see the benefit of separation of their twin children in the elementary school age. Usually, by first or second grade, twins have been separated in schools where such separation can be accommodated.

Parents may feel anxious prior to the beginning of a school year in which their twin children will be separated for the first time. The anxiety is confounded when one child is shyer and more emotionally dependent on the other. Parents may feel comfortable that the more outgoing child will fare well on his own and make friends easily but feel concerned about the child who is more reserved and withdrawn. The transition will almost always be harder for one child than the other. Imagine, however, how parents of a shy singleton would feel. They too are worried that their child might not feel at ease in his first days of school. Parents are all in the same boat in this regard. Children tend to be more resilient than parents think, and most parents will tell you that any trauma experienced during those first days is more acutely felt by the projecting parents than the child himself.

## Codependence

Some twin interviewees who stayed in the same class during junior high were happy to have been kept together. They felt that junior high was such a difficult time socially that it was good to have someone who could help you through those times. Psychologists might conclude that such a sentiment shows an unhealthy codependency between the twins. An adolescent generally needs to navigate tricky issues on her own to truly grow as an adult. If this growth from separation happens so late in life, imagine how difficult separation will be when it finally occurs.

Separation in school is a break from that emotional codependence that could be developing during the substantial amount of time the twins are not in school. In other words, emotional codependence could develop at an alarming rate in the twins' lives. The seven hours of the day that a child is in school is an opportunity to temper that development so that each child has a chance to grow his own sense of self and emotional independence.

There were many twins who reported that they reacted to separation differently than their siblings. Some dreaded separation, while others looked forward to it. Parents tend to gain a sense for which child will adjust better to separation and will have to gauge when the separation should occur and how to comfort the child for whom separation is more difficult.

A psychologist who is also a mother of twins advises to determine the timing of the separation based on the emotional maturity of your children. If separation would be overly traumatic for either child, wait to separate until the children are at least able to identify their emotions and can attempt to regulate them; generally, this occurs at four years of age or older.

## Social

Studies show that twins generally receive higher scores than singletons in socioemotional behaviors. Leadership and popularity were noted to be higher in the twin subjects than the non-twin counterparts. It is logical to conclude that twins generally have a head start over their singleton counterparts in socializing because they are forced to socialize with their twin, a peer of the same age, sooner than singletons are forced to socialize with any peers.

So much of a child's social development occurs in the school setting. Friends are made, cliques are formed, hierarchies are established, and friendships are challenged by a host of factors, including loyalty, popularity, perceptions of coolness, hobbies, and interests. Rare (if nonexistent) is the child who breezes through school

As adults, twins—particularly those who attend colleges and/or grad schools in different cities—can benefit from a double network of both social and business contacts. Friends and colleagues give the instant benefit of the doubt to the twin they haven't met yet, with the foundation laid by the first twin. Twin interviewees commented on how wonderful it was to have an expanded network of friends and potential business partners simply by having a co-twin who created his own book of contacts when he went off to a different college or to live in a different city.

without suffering from the trauma of one or more of these challenges. Social issues are often the number one reason for a child's
poor performance in school. The ability to concentrate and learn
in class can be significantly affected by the distraction of a devas-
tating (as perceived) social issue.

A person's character often takes shape in these formative
moments. Non-twin children tend to experience these moments
individually and enjoy deep personal growth while learning to
navigate and overcome social challenges. Twins, however, often
experience these moments together.

So while twins may socialize earlier than their singleton counterparts, they face a disadvantage in the formative social moments
by having a sibling of the same age and in the same social circle.
Imagine how much more the disadvantage is felt in the school
setting where twins are not separated. School could be the one
opportunity to allow the child to figure out where she stands
in the social pecking order and how she is going to respond to
threats to her social stature. But in schools where twins are placed
in the same classroom, that opportunity is lost.

Twin interviewees Brenda and Eleanor were in a small paro-
chial school growing up. Brenda recalls begging her mom to send
her to a separate school by eighth grade. "I needed a break from
being a twin," she explained. "Nothing happened in particular.
It's just that girls that age are very mean and I felt like I had to
bring Eleanor along, but my friends didn't want to hang out with
her. I felt like I had to have her back all the time."

In Eleanor's interview, she also acknowledged how hard those
years were: "I knew Brenda thought I was a burden, and I hated
that. I just didn't know how to break from the cycle because I
didn't really have my own friends."

Identical twin Shari echoed the sentiment that the middle and
high school years presented many social challenges. "There were

definitely times that I didn't like being half of a twin set," she said. "Sometimes I'd feel guilty because there was a part of me that wished I could know what it was like to just be me."

## Language

There are studies that document the disproportionate language deficits in twins compared to their non-twin counterparts. Twins—in particular, male twins—show delayed or diminished development in language and in verbal cognitive tasks compared to singletons. Between monozygotic and dizygotic twins, it is the former group that shows inferior language development to the latter in both genders. This difference may relate to the propensity for monozygotic twins to have been prematurely born and have lower birthrates than dizygotic twins.

Outside of incidences related to birth, there are various factors for language delays in twins:

- Twins have reduced verbal interaction with parents and caregivers because the attention a parent might otherwise have given to a singleton child is divided in half.
- Because of the difficulty for a single caregiver to transport twin infants to different locations, twins often have less social interaction and fewer social opportunities outside of the twinship in the early months and years of life.
- Many twins form their own private language (referred to by scientists as *idioglossia*) that only they can speak and understand.
- Having your peer understand you reduces the feeling of urgency in communicating with others that a singleton child might feel. Gone is the incentive to quickly learn to speak the language of the rest of the world.

One way teachers can try to avoid confusion, as some identical twin interviewees reported, is to create seating assignments where each identical twin occupies opposite sides of the classroom. The teachers would just set to memory which twin was on which side of the room.

It should be noted that studies indicate that even though language may be delayed in the first eighteen to twenty-four months of twins' lives, their speech proficiency usually evens out with that of their non-twin peers by thirty-six months. Studies also demonstrate that separately-placed twins showed more advanced speech comprehension and usage than twins who were placed together.

## Academic

Studies of twins in the school setting yielded notable findings with regard to twins who were separated. Twins who were separated, for instance, showed greater differences in their intellectual ability than twins who were kept in the same classroom. As one might presume, monozygotic twins tended to show more similarity in general intelligence, learning challenges, school achievement, and temperament in the classroom setting than dizygotic twins.

Some schools have mandatory separation policies for siblings. Some twins reported that so intent were the schools and parents on separating them that one twin of a pair would wind up in a different (and inappropriate) learning track because class sizes were too small to place both twins in different classes in the same learning track. Most educators agree that this type of forced separation is detrimental; the separation of twins should not be prioritized over proper tracking for academic aptitude. Educators also seemed to agree that for English as a Second Language (ESL) students, it was often beneficial and/or necessary to keep twins together.

Some twins who were separated in high school still wound up in some of the same classes because there was only one of that class. For instance, in senior year, there was only one Advanced Placement history class offered.

For identical twins, a commonly voiced concern was not receiving proper credit for class participation. Teachers showed obvious inability to distinguish one twin from the other, and each was left to wonder how the teacher was able to accurately assign a grade for class participation to each student.

One twin interviewee, Florence, reported having performed a mini monologue in her high school Spanish class and receiving an evaluation that was clearly written for her identical twin sister, who also had to do the monologue. "My mom went into the school and screamed at the teacher," she recalled. "I was so embarrassed at the time, but in retrospect, I think it's good that she did that. It was good to have an advocate who would fight for us to be individuals."

For both identical and fraternal twins, even when there was no confusion as to who was who, many individuals complained that teachers would compare them, and being in the same class-room compounded this problem.

Sometimes, the academic needs of the twin children conflict with their social and emotional needs. For instance, if the twins' birthdates are close enough to the cut-off date, parents are often given the choice whether to place their children in the year ahead so they'll be among the youngest in the grade or to hold them back so that they are among the oldest in the grade. One twin may be much more academically advanced than the other; she may do better being pushed a year ahead while the other twin may do better staying back. Rare is the parent who will agree to place each child where she does best academically when it means placing them in different grades. More common is the parent who will value the emotional and social benefits of staying in the same grade over the academic benefits of going to different grades.

Special education teachers seem to have less difficulty encouraging a sense of individuality in their twin students, regardless of whether they were kept in the same class. Special education teachers have to regularly compose Individual Education Programs (IEPs) for each student. They are constantly considering the individual strengths of a student and catering to his specific learning needs. These educators are so trained in individualizing each student that they rarely confuse or compare one twin student to another. The biggest challenge for special education teachers relating to twin students is managing parent expectations. Parents generally have trouble recognizing how distinct the learning needs of each child are and resist recommendations for IEPs that are different for each child. Special education educators tend to wish for IEP discussions to be scheduled for each child on different days (not back-to-back, which is most convenient for the parents) so that the parents are able to focus solely on the consideration of one child without the distracting and generally unhelpful comparison to the other.

Another issue in keeping twin children together that tends to manifest in the later years is cheating. Identical twins, in particular, have faced accusations of cheating more frequently than fraternal twins. But all twins, in general, tend to be accused of cheating more than their non-twin peers. Genetic similarities or similarity in upbringing can result in similar answers on exams, leading teachers to inaccurately conclude that the twins were somehow colluding with one another. (Of course, sometimes the accusation of cheating is not inaccurate and the twins have, in fact, colluded. Not YOUR children, of course; other twin children . . .)

## College Years

About a quarter of the twins I interviewed attended the same college or university as their co-twins. Very few of them roomed together, and they found that having separate living space in college allowed them to have some freedom from each other, learn how to live with another individual, and make different friends from one another. Very few of the twins I interviewed who went to the same college pursued the same major and thus did not have to take the same courses. The college years, therefore, were a time when most twins, whether in the same college or not, could enjoy an opportunity to grow separately.

For all the twins I interviewed who went to different colleges, the experience was overall very positive. Some mentioned that the first semester of college was the most difficult as they adjusted to daily life without their twin sibling. It was a new and interesting experience for twins returning home from the first school break to have to spend more time reconnecting and filling each other in on roommates, professors, campus, and classes. Many twin interviewees also commented that they realized how close their relationship with one another was when they separated for the college years.

Another new experience for twins who separate for the first time during college is the chance to introduce one's twin status at her own leisure. Each twin can present herself as, for example, "Courtney" instead of "one half of the Smith Twins." This ability to be someone new for the first time can be both anxiety producing and thrilling. At this point in their lives, some twins may not know what it's like to be a person whose own singular existence has great importance.

Twins who develop their own friendships separate from that of their twin siblings enjoy growing their collective group of friends. And in cases where the twins have a strong relationship and bond, the college-age friends of one twin usually embrace the other twin as one of their own.

Of course, from the parents' perspective, having one's twin children in two different colleges can prove to be a logistical challenge, especially when the schools' schedules (for moving in, moving out, graduation, etc.) present a conflict. One set of triplets with whom I spoke had their three separate graduation ceremonies on the same weekend. With a tight and meticulously coordinated schedule, each parent had to travel by plane separately across the country to ensure that at least one of them was at each child's ceremony. The positive: each child had one parent at his graduation. The negative: both parents were not able to enjoy every child's graduation ceremony, denying every child the opportunity to be celebrated by both parents at such an important milestone. It was also unfortunate that each child was not able to celebrate his sibling's own accomplishment. Needless to say, parents and their children need to think outside the box and find creative ways to make sure that each child's individual accomplishments during these years are celebrated fully.

## Effect on the Future

Some twin interviewees who were not separated early in school reported having difficulty adjusting when they were older and became full-time employees at a job. From early on, twins are part of a team. Often, this team gangs up on other siblings, classmates, and even parents. As part of the team, the teammates learn quickly how to collaborate and make decisions that affect not the parts alone but the sum of the parts. Twins tend to be accustomed to collective decision-making and taking into account others' feelings and needs when deciding how to move forward. Constantly thinking "in the collective" can make an individual a great team player in the workplace. Sometimes, however, the collective mentality can hinder one's independence and personal growth. As adults, twins who were accustomed to collaborative thinking had to learn to make decisions on their own, without input from, or concern for, others. Perhaps parents can help twins who grow up with a collective way of thinking to evaluate how they prefer working and whether changing their mindsets or alternating teamwork approaches might improve their productivity and success in the office.

## Bottom Line: To Separate or Not?

Even the strongest proponents of ensuring your twin children maintain separate identities and life experiences advocate for a child-tailored approach to the separation issue. They recommend that while separation is preferred as a general rule, every rule has exceptions, and whether (and when) to separate twins should be determined on a case-by-case basis. One position united all the twins, teachers, administrators, and psychologists whom I consulted: separation should absolutely not be mandated by law or policy.

## Tips for Deciding Whether to Separate

- School placement decisions should be a collaborative effort among administrators, teachers, and parents. They should be based upon the special and unique circumstances of each twin and not the result of a one-size-fits-all policy.

- Observe your twin children in preschool or nursery school so you can gain a sense of the level of their emotional and social codependency.

- Schedule parent-teacher conferences on different days, if possible, or in time slots that are not contiguous. Resist the temptation to bring up the other child as a point of comparison.

- Do not push your twin children to apply to the same college, even if it would be logistically easier and less expensive for you.

- If there's a mandatory separation policy in your school, seek out the local chapter of the national activist group that is fighting mandatory separation policies with legislation.

## Tips for Twins in the Same Classroom

- Discuss with the teacher opportunities for separation, such as group projects.

- Request that the twins are seated far apart from one another to reduce the appearance of cheating (and to help teachers identify which one is which).

- Ensure that the teacher knows the distinct educational needs of each child and does not expressly or indirectly compare the two to each other.

- If you or your children suspect that a grade or penalty was given in error (i.e., to the wrong child), bring it up immediately with the teacher and/or administrators and help develop a game plan for ensuring that it doesn't happen again.

- In the case of identical twins, help the teacher develop quick visual cues to distinguish one child from the other.
- Speak openly and frequently with your children to make sure they feel that they are being treated fairly and individually.
- Encourage some alone time and separation for your twin children outside of school—socially and with extra-curricular activities.

# CHAPTER EIGHT

# Prepare Them for Other Relationships

*Love outside of the twinship
doesn't work that way.*

—Josh

**B**eing a twin has an effect on relationships outside the twinship, including romantic relationships and close friendships. I was fascinated to read various data and studies about twins and relationships and even more tickled to hear from twins themselves as to the complicated relationship conundrums they experienced.

# Romantic Relationships

There is data that demonstrates that twins tend to marry later in life than singletons. Some researchers conclude this is because twins are so emotionally close with one another that their need to find that bond in other partners is not as great as it is for singletons. Other researchers posit that the heritability of propensity to marry (or lack thereof) is the cause for the discrepancy.

From my interviews, it appeared that many twins face certain challenges when trying to find a partner that non-twins typically don't encounter. When growing up with an around-the-clock playdate, study buddy, partner in crime, and best friend, it is hard to develop an intimate and close relationship with someone outside of the twin relationship. The bond is so strong between a close set of twins that it is hard for them to imagine being able to have a strong bond with someone else. Some twins described their emotional attachment as adults as "childlike." And many twins noted that they felt their twin relationship was stronger and deeper than their parents' marriage.

Some twin interviewees actually described their relationships as quasi-marriages, at least for the first eighteen years of their lives. They collectively made decisions, nurtured a partnership, fought, made up, and traveled together—they did everything married couples do outside of physical, sexual intimacy.

Zameera works with her fraternal twin sister in their parents' restaurant. They spend almost the entire day together for five days out of every week. When I asked how spending so much time together has affected their relationship, Zameera responded, "Oh, we definitely would get on each other's nerves. But we promised each other that at the end of every night, no matter how much we fought during the day, we'd always say 'goodnight' and 'I love you.' You know, you never want to go to bed angry." As you know, *Don't go to bed angry* is arguably the most cliché piece of marital advice, and Zameera and her twin sister made a commitment to each other to comply with it.

In a 2016 *Guardian* article featuring twins Antony and Richard, Antony recalled, "It's hard to describe how close we are. When I got married, my wife and I came home from honeymoon and spent our first night in our new house together. I remember lying in bed and it finally hit me that I was never going to be in the same house as Rich again. I'd just married the love of my life, but I couldn't help thinking, *What the hell am I doing? I should be at home with Rich.* I didn't sleep at all that night."[1]

Adrian and her twin sister lived in a small three-bedroom house. Their mother had one bedroom, there was a tiny "uninhabitable" bedroom, and Adrian and her sister shared the third bedroom. After high school, Adrian's sister moved out of the house to live with their grandmother. "It was liberating at first: no one was eating my ice cream or taking over the TV remote. I was like, *This is all mine.*" But then Adrian started to feel lonely. She missed having someone to talk to about her day. And she hated watching television alone.

I asked Adrian which was better: sharing her space with her sister (and putting up with the division of goods) or having her own space (and managing the loneliness). Adrian immediately chose the former. She explained, "I'm not sure it has to be my sister, necessarily. I just know that I want to be with someone at the end of the day, someone to talk to, someone to be with. I think because I grew up with a twin, I have a harder time being alone. It always feels like something is missing—like some*one* is missing."

Twins Sander and Carter sing in a popular folk duo together. They have been each other's best friends their entire lives, and when they sing together, it's seamless. When they've tried to introduce other band members, it's been a challenge. Sander recounted, "Being a twin made it hard to communicate with others. With Carter, I don't have to say anything. He just knows what I'm thinking, so I never need to tell him. And I forget that not everyone else is in my head like Carter. So I need to use my words, but I'm not used to doing that."

Carter, in a separate interview, said, "When we're singing, I can give Sander a look and he knows what I mean and he knows what to do next. But when you work with others, you can't rely on that. So when I have to collaborate with someone else, there's always a struggle—it's so much more effort."

Researchers have noted that twins tend to project their twinship onto other significant relationships; it has been referred to as "twin yearning." For twins who are so close that they only know what it is like to feel attached to another person and to feel part of a set, they typically seek a life partner who can essentially comprise the other half of their identity.

Studies have shown that twins do not end up choosing respective long-term partners who are similar to each other. In fact, when asked to rate the partner chosen by their identical twin sibling, 95 percent of subjects said that they could have never fallen in love with their co-twin's mate, while 38 percent plainly disliked that person.

A 2015 segment on NBC's *Today Show* featured well-known twins Jenna Bush Hager and Barbara Bush, former President George W. Bush's daughters. They discussed their deep bond, that they were each other's best friends in childhood, and that they continue to be so throughout their adulthood. They joked that their sense of humor is unique to them and that few others understand it, especially Jenna's husband, Henry. Jenna laughed, "I mean, Henry rolls his eyes at us a lot, don't you think?" Barbara nodded her head and acknowledged that Henry is affected by their close connection. Barbara commented, "He got me in the marriage also . . . I think he's had to take a number of naps with both of us, and that might get annoying." Jenna assured Barbara that Henry really doesn't mind. "He says he's the ham in the ham sandwich."[2]

Twin interviewees told me that they were disappointed to learn that other people typically do not deliver the unconditional love and mutual understanding to which they had grown accustomed with their twin. "Love outside of the twinship doesn't work that way," commented interviewee Josh. Twins are surprised to learn that they might have to make personality or behavioral changes in order to make the relationship work, whereas they were allowed to be themselves and act as they always acted in their dealings with their twin siblings. General aphorisms like "love isn't easy" or "love takes work" don't always seem to apply in the deep relationship that twins develop between themselves—a relationship where love is unconditional and unquestioned. "With [my twin sibling], I don't have to work so hard to be understood," reported one interviewee. It is thus a shock to many twins' systems when they learn that love outside of the twinship works differently. Significant relationship success outside the twinship generally takes effort.

When a twin does find love, he encounters other problems figuring out who he is as a partner and the role his partner is supposed to play in his life. When a twin marries his partner, she is supposed to also be his best friend, but he may still have that deep, long-standing connection with his twin. Sometimes, it is difficult to effectively explain the intensity of the twin relationship to his spouse if she is not a twin herself. Even though the twin is emotionally close with his partner, he still has that undeniable connection with his co-twin. This dynamic rears its proverbial head particularly in times of important moments in an adult twin's life. The adult twin has to determine who is "number one" in his life. For instance, whom does a twin call first when he loses his job—his co-twin or his partner?

Twins have known each other deeply for their whole lives, while their spouses have known them for significantly less time. Some twin interviewees expressed feelings of guilt when a partner would call them their "best friend" because the twin felt that her only true best friend was her twin sibling. Interviewees explained that their putative partners needed to come into the relationship with an understanding that there was another individual that they had a very intimate relationship with and that the relationship would continue to grow over time along with the new partner relationship.

Twin interviewee Patrick and his wife, Melanie, faced a significant hurdle in their relationship that required them to seek help from their clerical advisor, who does relationship counseling. Patrick and his twin brother, Shane, had a tight bond to which Melanie could not relate. Patrick had told Melanie about a special memory he had from childhood. From the age of four years old, Patrick and Shane would spend every other weekend at their great uncle's house. Their great uncle would take them to the woodsy area behind his house to teach them how to identify different birds or to the nearby park to teach them how to throw a Frisbee.

Patrick and Shane loved spending time with their great uncle but also enjoyed walks alone on a long path, which led to a huge tree. They would take the long, windy walk to the big tree every month or so. They referred to this tree as "our tree." When they were fifteen years old, they carved their initials into the tree. The following year, their great uncle died, and thus ended the regular tradition of visiting their tree. During their college years, when drunkenly reminiscing about their great uncle, his house, and their tree, Patrick and Shane got tattoos on their arms of the tree with their initials on it.

Not long after Patrick and Melanie started dating, Melanie noticed the tree tattoo but decided against asking Patrick about it until they had been dating five or six months. When she finally asked Patrick about it, he recounted his fond memories with Shane at their great uncle's house. A year later, Patrick and Melanie became engaged and Melanie asked Patrick if he would take her to this special tree; Patrick felt uncomfortable and said no.

"We had a huge fight about it," Patrick reported. "We almost didn't go through with the wedding, which is why we had to see that counselor. I just felt like she was out of place to ask me that. It was like she was inviting herself into this very sacred thing that I shared alone with Shane."

Years later, Patrick and Melanie are happily married, but they don't seem to have resolved this festering issue. Patrick is certain that he will never take Melanie (or anyone) to his and Shane's tree, and Melanie, who has decided not to push the issue further, still feels entitled to see it.

Studies have confirmed that there often exists a rivalry between spouse and co-twin. Researchers have concluded that the conflict arises when twins are emotionally codependent on one another and have difficulty with anyone who intentionally or unintentionally threatens the inter-twin attachment. Twins have an easier time finding and bonding with partners when their relationship with their twin is close but independent as opposed to close but dependent.

Identical twins Eli and Gabe, for instance, have always been emotionally close. They went to the same college but pursued different graduate degrees in different cities, which is when Eli met his wife, Malka. Eli reported that what made this particular relationship work was that Malka understood the tight relationship between Eli and his brother. She was one of the only women Eli had dated who did not feel the need to compete with Gabe for Eli's attention and affection. She was comfortable with, and admiring of, the close relationship between the brothers. She jokingly tells friends that Eli calls Gabe to tell him what he ate for dinner that evening.

For Brian and his twin, they talk about everything except for one topic—sexual encounters. That topic is avoided to prevent jealousy, but not for the reason you'd think. Brian explained, "We share everything with each other, but not about our hookups. It seems like that could lead to some jealousy—and not jealousy as in wanting to be with that girl too. Jealousy as in the idea that someone might come along and take your place as the most important person in their life."

In studies on marriage quality and twinships, twins are not more likely to divorce than singletons and, in the event of divorce, the dissolution of marriage is more often caused by infidelity of a spouse than competition between spouse and co-twin. Such studies also demonstrate that the most harmonious marriages for twins who share a close bond are those where the twins' respective spouses were related or friendly to each other before either one married one of the twins.

In a way, having a twin prepares adults for serious relationships. One twin interviewee relayed that she purposely chose a marital partner who had different strengths from her because she was used to balancing positive traits this way, as she did with her twin brother growing up. Other twins mentioned that they are very comfortable with physical intimacy and closeness because from conception, they were physically close to another body.

In a poignant essay in the *Pennsylvania Gazette*, Daniel Blas describes how he managed living with his three sisters in one bedroom as a child. Some nights he would listen to the Yankees game on his Walkman radio. He described the comfort he felt when he would hear the fifty thousand screaming fans and could create a mental space of his own. "The play-by-play, public to the world, was private to me." Or when reading in his bunk bed, sometimes he would break out in laughter. When his sister in the bunk below asked what was so funny, he would dismiss her and say, "You wouldn't get it." He said that "not because she wouldn't actually have understood, but because I wanted a semblance of solitude."[3]

Twins, too, need to be creative in the way they find personal mental space, and by doing so, they can enjoy the close physicality of having someone always there without the suffocation that could result from having perpetual company.

Twins' comfort with physical closeness can also have negative consequences for the twin in a serious relationship. Being accustomed to and comforted by having close physical contact can also manifest in a discomfort of being alone for any length of time. As Isabelle explained, "Because I

In an interview with triplet Devon, I learned that triplets might not have the same difficulty that twins generally face in forming bonds with significant others. Devon is very close with her triplet sisters as well as the other sibling in their family. She said that finding partners in life was never a struggle and the ability to develop a close relationship with another was not affected by the fact that she was a triplet. When we discussed why this is, she suggested that because there were always at least three of them together at any given time, there was seldom an opportunity to build a strong one-on-one bond with any one sibling. So it's not out of the realm of reason to conclude that triplets, counterintuitively, might be more similar to a singleton than to a twin with regard to forming close relationships with non-siblings.

had my twin sister near me at all times growing up, I now have a significant dislike of being alone, and that was a challenge for my husband, who is just one of those people who needs space from time to time. I have trouble understanding his need to be alone, so I smother him, he says—and he doesn't understand why I never want or need that space for myself."

In an NPR TED Radio Hour segment, couples' therapist and author Esther Perel dismissed the popular claim that spouses are each other's best friends. She explained, "Many people treat their partners in ways they would never treat their best friends. And [they] allow themselves to say and do things that no best friend would ever accept. Friendship does not operate along the same lines [as marriage]."[4]

So are close twin relationships more like an abuse-prone marriage or more like a typical best friendship?

Many twins told me that they love their twin unconditionally and can often treat them (or allow themselves to be treated) poorly. "Our close friends are shocked by how mean we are to each other. But it's okay with us. That's how we are. We are brutally honest with one another. Now we would never talk to anyone else like that. But with your twin sister, it's okay to just say it straight up. She will never leave you, she will never stop loving you. And she will give it back to you when you deserve it." Many of my interviewees said their relationship is more like a marriage in the openness, comfort level, and ability to rip into one another when the moment requires.

But I wonder if the comparison is actually so clear cut. Look at the other relationships in twins' lives. Friends come in and out of a twin's life. Parents are there in the beginning, but they leave early. Spouses are there until the end, but they arrive late. A twin, however, is there the entire time—from the beginning until the end.

So maybe a close twin relationship mimics neither a best friendship nor a marital partnership. It resides in its own category. It encompasses unconditional love, a long history of shared experiences, freedom to be oneself, and a deep, deep knowledge and understanding of the other person. It is an intimacy like no other.

# Close Friendship

Another category of relationships that is affected by twinships is the platonic friendship. Interestingly, studies show that twins advance past the parallel play stage of infancy more quickly than their singleton peers because they have much more practice sharing space and toys with another individual. This result would seem to indicate that twins make friends with other children more easily than singletons do, but that is not necessarily the case.

Twins who have a very close relationship with each other might have trouble developing close friendships outside of the twinship. A twin already has a confidant and might not necessarily look for one in another friend. A twin might not have the same emotional needs as their close friends and might not engage in important giving and sharing moments in outside friendships, thus not developing closely with others. As a triplet interviewee stated, "I never had to find friends because I was born with my two closest friends. I never really extended myself in friendships outside of my brother and sister. I kind of limited myself simply because I didn't feel like anything was missing."

A twin interviewee told me that she never felt sad or disappointed to leave a friend's house after she and her twin sister were hanging out there. One of the best parts about being a twin was "getting to bring my best friend home with me all the time."

In Chapter One, I told the story of Cody, who lost her identical twin Teddi when they were in their twenties. Up until the day

Teddi died, she and Cody spoke every day on the phone. They were each other's best friend and had a deep connection. One of the hardest parts for Cody in adjusting to life without Teddi was in making close friends. "At first, it was just impossible to fill the void that I felt," Cody explained. "But then it just became clear that I didn't really know how to have a close friend or how to be a close friend to someone. I never really knew how to open up to someone because I never needed to. Teddi knew me so well, I never needed to talk about how I was feeling—she just knew."

Now, in her thirties, Cody is just starting to be able to have deep and emotionally fulfilling friendships with other women. She feels happier now that she can honestly say that she has close (and even "best") girlfriends, but she noted that she still cannot pick up the phone at 3:00 a.m. and call any of these women "the way I could with Teddi."

Many twins find it difficult to make friends simply because they don't know who they are as individuals. They don't know themselves outside of their twin identities. A particular problem expressed to me by some interviewees is that when twins are constantly hanging out in the same social circles, one twin cannot mold to other groups with different identities because the co-twin might "call him out" for not being genuine. As one twin reported, "I just couldn't go through what other kids went through in order to discover my identity because [my twin sister] was always around."

For fraternal twins Mohammed and Dari, Mohammed was more extroverted and Dari was shy. Dari tended to hang out with Mohammed and the friends Mohammed accumulated. For a time, Dari felt that they were all friends equally, but around high school, it became apparent that those friends were more like Mohammed and interested in him. Dari felt he had less and less in common with these friends and, therefore, felt as though something was wrong with him. Now that he's in his thirties, Dari can see that he simply did not have a lot in common with Mohammed's friends. They were interested in going to movies and hanging out with girls. Dari was more interested in playing sports and video games. It wasn't until his last year of high school that Dari realized he could have a separate group of friends and still be close with his brother.

A secret weapon in kids' arsenals is to attack another kid's weak spot. For twins, that weak spot is their co-twin. Indeed, sometimes a mean kid would engage in a very direct form of bullying: insulting one twin by stating that he liked the co-twin better. An insult to one's twin sibling is typically felt very acutely and personally by the other twin. As one twin said, "I wanted to tell them, 'Just say you like me without putting my twin down.'" In fact, multiple twins of varying backgrounds lamented that so-called friends had said "I like your sister better," "Your brother is more fun than you," and "Your sister is smarter." Having a co-twin thus exposes a twin to a particular brand of bullying not usually experienced by singletons.

Many twin interviewees felt guilt when certain individuals (for example, in the "popular crowd") would want to include them but not their twin sibling. It is a real dilemma for the included twin who wants the attention from the social group. Will the twin go along with the group in excluding her twin or will she risk alienation from the group by defending her co-twin?

I interviewed twins Brenda and Eleanor; Brenda, who was liked by a huge group of friends, stayed loyal to Eleanor and always invited her along despite the protests of her friends. But both Brenda and Eleanor reflect on those times with deep regret. Brenda feels like she didn't have a chance to enjoy her friends on her own, and Eleanor feels bad for having "weighed Brenda down."

Sometimes other kids compare twins to each other and assign funny names or other features to distinguish one from another. This typically leads to one twin being put down more than the other, which makes both children feel dejected. Twin interviewees reported that they felt constantly burdened by looking out for the other twin in social settings. For a set of male/female twins in high school, the male twin did not like seeing his sister date people he knew. He was less protective of her during the college years, when they attended universities in different cities.

But not all twins had negative experiences in the social circles of their younger years. Elaine and Joel enjoyed having different friends. Elaine was a "bookworm," had thick glasses, and always wanted to hang out in the library. Joel was a "jock," very athletic,

Another factor complicating friendships for twins is that some relationships might develop out of the friend's fascination with the twinship. In some communities where twins are rare, they often experience a sort of celebrity status. People are excited by them and want to know them better so they can gain an understanding of an area in which they have little or no experience. But if your twin children become popular simply because of their status as twins, they will soon feel devalued as individuals.

For young children, if a twin child perceives that it is the twinship and not her individual characteristics that attract a friend, she might mistakenly believe that her only value as a friend or person is limited to her status as a twin. A child should feel as though she is being liked for her unique traits. It's important for parents of young children to guide them in their social relationships and ensure that friends are expressing interest in being together for the right reasons.

and liked playing outside. Many of Elaine's friends had "secret crushes" on Joel, and Joel's friends were accepting of Elaine; they admired her intelligence and treated her kindly. Both Elaine and Joel reported that they believe their friends were so nice to the other twin because they knew the twins wouldn't have tolerated the alternative. Joel said of his friends, "They knew better than to make fun of Elaine in front of me."

When it came time for college, many twin interviewees who went to separate schools felt the need to be exceptionally social. Many told me they disliked the feeling of being alone and the quietness it brought. It felt foreign to not have someone around constantly. One twin interviewee expressed having an "intolerance for solitude," so she would go out of her way to fill her time with social events. Other twin interviewees welcomed the change and enjoyed the adventure of feeling like a singleton for once—being socially free, not having to adjust their social behaviors to accommodate their co-twins, and, yes, enjoying some peace and quiet.

Many twins also reported that they loved having their twin siblings visit them for the weekend. In some cases, this was the first time they revealed to their friends that they were one half of a twinship, which always seemed to surprise and delight friends who otherwise thought they knew them so well. In almost all the cases, the visiting twin felt very welcomed by the hosting twin's friends. "I didn't have to prove myself like I would in any other setting," one interviewee observed. "I was just accepted and loved simply because I was 'the twin sister.'"

Researchers studying the "twin yearning" phenomenon noted that it affected not only twins seeking romantic relationships but twins seeking platonic friends as well. The twin looks for an individual who can comprise "my other half." Usually, twins are unsuccessful in their attempts to find friends who can fill the role that their twins have occupied. Twins generally have fewer physical and emotional boundaries than non-twins due to growing up in such close physical proximity to their twin. Talking or standing too close can be off-putting to non-twins who have never shared space or time to the same degree with another peer. Twins who are trying to find another twin when seeking social friends may exhibit other maladaptive behavior, complicating the quality of friendships. Notably, monozygotic twins demonstrate more twin yearning than dizygotic twins.

## Tips for Helping Twins Develop Healthy Relationships Outside the Twinship

- Encourage your children to pursue different interests and activities (which will expose them to different friends).
- When your children are young, schedule separate play-dates for them.
- Give each child his own play space, if not his own bedroom.
- Discuss social dynamics with teachers; they are often in a better position than you to observe any unhealthy behavior between your twins.
- Remind your twin children that others are not always as accustomed to sharing toys and space as your twin children are with each other.
- Teach your twins to be patient and understanding of their peers who do not necessarily behave in the same ways that they do.
- Encourage your children's friends (and their parents) to communicate the distinct qualities that solidify the friendship.

- For adult children, encourage open dialogue about challenges they face in finding and maintaining healthy relationships outside of the twinship. Be supportive of their choices and gently guide them in their non-twin relationships.
- There are support groups for parents of twins and for twins themselves. These may be helpful resources in dealing with relationship problems that commonly arise in twins.

1. Pook, "'I've Never Needed Anyone Else'."

2. Eun Kyung Kim, "Jenna Bush Hager, Sister Barbara Bush Share Secrets of Being a Twin," Today.com, June 22, 2015, https://www.today.com/health/jenna-bush-hager-sister-barbara-share-secrets-being-twins-t27756.

3. Daniel Blas, "Four's Company," *The Pennsylvania Gazette*, June 24, 2015, http://thepenngazette.com/fours-company/.

4. Esther Perel in an interview with Guy Raz, "Are We Asking Too Much of Our Spouses?" *National Public Radio*'s TED Radio Hour, April 25, 2014, http://www.npr.org/templates/transcript/transcript.php?storyId=301825600.

# CHAPTER NINE

# Final Thoughts

They didn't seem to understand
what I was going through.

—Jocelyn

I f there is one underlying piece of advice that one can string through each chapter of advice in this book, it's that you should shift your perspective to that of your child. If you tried to put yourself in your child's shoes and walk around a little, you would gain a deep understanding of his perspective. You would see his twin sibling through his own eyes. You would see yourself and the world around you reacting to the other twin. You would better understand the frustrations with having the social obligations of a twin. And you would better understand the jealousy of watching a co-twin succeed when you haven't.

You could empathize with the need for space from a twin and the desire for special one-on-one time with you. Every chapter in this book highlights the need for us as parents to try to view the world through the eyes of our children.

And if there's one piece of parenting advice that has helped me immensely in dealing with twin-related, or simply child-related, conflict, it's that you should validate first. Your children's emotions are raw and real. If they're running high, your child won't be able to hear the logic and reason you are trying to impart upon them. Validating helps your child feel understood and helps their brain shift from emotional to rational.

Below are explanations and examples of each of the above pieces of advice. I urge you to try these; really, really try these. I feel confident they will help you resolve conflicts more smoothly.

# Perspective Shifting

One of my favorite scenes from the movie *Annie Hall* is when Annie and her partner Alvy Singer are in sessions with their respective analysts. There's a split screen so the viewer can see both patients as they answer their analysts' questions. When asked how often they have sex, Alvy tells his analyst, "Hardly ever. Maybe three times a week." Annie tells her analyst, "Constantly! I'd say three times a week."[1]

Clearly, whether three times per week is "hardly ever" or "constantly" is a matter of perspective. And if two anxious, charming, humorous, insecure New Yorkers who are in an intimate relationship can have opposing perspectives, imagine how often you and your very different children of an entirely different generation do!

A video that went viral in 2017 poignantly displayed the very different perspective a child can have from that of a parent. In "A

Normal Day," a husband comes home at the end of the day and asks his wife how her day was. The video then shows a montage of all the things she is recalling from her day: her toddler stealing a toy from her baby sister and causing the baby to scream; the kids crying as they're buckled into their car seats; a trip to the supermarket where the baby knocks several rolls of toilet paper off the shelf; and then, back at home, the toddler dropping a plate full of cake onto the floor. After the montage, she sighs and says, "So yeah, it was just a normal day."

Then, as the father is tucking the toddler into bed, he asks her how her day was. There's another montage—this time from the child's perspective. It shows her hugging her baby sister, getting a kiss from her mother when being buckled into the car seat, laughing as she's sitting in the grocery cart and her mom runs as she pushes it through the parking lot, and then sitting on the kitchen floor with her mom eating the smashed cake. She concludes, "It was the best day ever!"[2] (If you are not crying now, go watch the video. Then try not crying. I dare you.) Can you think of an instance where your perspective of an event differed significantly from that of your child? If not, then you probably need to give more thought to how your child sees the world.

In *The Ultimate Guide to Raising Teens and Tweens: Strategies for Unlocking Your Child's Full Potential*, Douglas Haddad suggests that parents perform an exercise to help them connect to their teenage children. He lists several questions designed to help the reader rekindle specific feelings from her past life as a child.[3] In other words, after spending time reflecting on your own childhood and how you liked and didn't like your experiences as a teen, you can gain a better understanding of what your teenage children are going through. I loved this idea: to really understand your children, get in their heads!

Parents of twins can use this methodology for gaining insight into what their twin children are experiencing. After all, most parents of twins are not twins themselves, but they can still attempt to gain a deeper understanding of their children's lives as twins. They can consider:

- How would I feel if I had to share a room in middle school?
- How would I feel if my friend was having a party and I wasn't invited to it but my sister was?
- Would I enjoy being dressed like my sibling every day?
- How would I feel if no one seemed to want to take a photo of me alone without someone else in the frame?
- How would I feel if someone I really liked showed more of an interest in my brother than in me?
- How would I feel if a coach questioned my athletic ability in comparison to that of another family member?
- Would I enjoy having a sidekick?
- Would I take comfort in knowing that someone my age always had my back?

For parents of twins who also have non-twin children, they can ask themselves additional questions like:

- What would it be like to have two siblings who are very close to each other?
- Would I feel comfortable as the "third wheel"?
- How would I feel if it seemed like everyone in the family (except for me) had a partner?
- Would I feel disempowered if I didn't have someone advocating for my needs the way my twin siblings advocate for each other?
- What if people always wanted to talk to me about my twin siblings?

It behooves us as parents to try to get into our children's heads. Think about what is troubling them, what is making them happy, and how they reflect on their experiences. According to Dr. Laura Markham, understanding the world from your child's perspective can calm a tantrum, avert a meltdown, reverse a child's anger toward you, get a misbehaving child to listen to you, and help transition your child through major milestones like potty training, first-day-of-school jitters, and a teen's quest for independence.[4]

# Validation

A not-unrelated principle of modern parenting is validation. Karyn Hall and Melissa Cook, in *The Power of Validation: Arming Your Child against Bullying, Peer Pressure, Addiction, Self-Harm & Out-of-Control Emotions*, define validation as "offer[ing] acceptance and feedback about the other person's reality in a nonjudgmental way."[5] When we validate our children, we're not necessarily agreeing with their conclusions. But we are allowing our children to feel the way they do. We are accepting them for who they are in every moment. The message they receive is that we love them no matter what feelings and thoughts they have.

When my five-year-old daughter Tal did not feel competent in a dance class, she had a meltdown in the hallway. Through her sobs, she said, "Eden is a winner, and I'm a loser." I hated the words she was using (Where did she learn the word *loser* anyway?), and I responded with my gut. "Don't ever say that!" I hissed. I told her that I never wanted to hear her say those words again because they're not true, and no one is a loser, and what a terrible word to have in one's vocabulary, etc.

What I failed to do was validate her feelings. I reacted viscerally rather than mindfully. I felt so urgently that her thought was "wrong" that I attacked it in the instant. I showed her that I did not approve of her feelings and interpretations of the situation. I communicated, in part, that I did not accept her in that moment.

As counterintuitive as it would have been, I should have told her that I understood that she was upset about her dancing. That I, too, might feel less competent if I wasn't able to master a certain skill right away. Maybe I could have told her a story of when I felt disappointed in my perceived lack of talent, and—if this wouldn't lead too far afield—I could explain that, with practice, I improved. The point is, I should have met her where she was—feeling sad—rather than immediately chastising her for the language she was using to express her sadness.

Many twin interviewees referenced a lack of validation. When Jocelyn would complain to her parents about her sister's behavior, her parents would immediately dismiss her concerns. Jocelyn reported, "They would always say something like, 'Why are you complaining? You are so lucky to have your best friend with you at all times! None of your other friends get to share a room with their best friend or have sleepovers every night.' It was like I wasn't allowed to ever be unhappy being a twin because, according to them, I was so lucky. When I got older, I would feel guilty when I was unhappy with my twin sister or how she treated me—like I should be more grateful for my situation." Jocelyn's words are telling: her parents didn't *allow* her to be unhappy, to have the feelings she had. Without that validation in those early years, Jocelyn learned that her feelings of dissatisfaction with her twin sister were not justified. And if a child feels that a parent won't approve of her feelings, why open up to the parent at all?

Thus, if you want your kids to be expressive and open with you, provide them a nonjudgmental and safe space to release their feelings and their thoughts. First, let them vent. Then validate. Then discuss. Of course, resolving your children's behavior or other problems is not always that simple. But sometimes it is. So it's worth a try every time.

# Final Thoughts

About a quarter of the twins I interviewed felt that their parents did a great job raising them. "You should talk to my parents," they'd say, because, as far as they were concerned, their parents did everything right. I felt admiring of those parents. To have grateful children—what a blessing! If my children are anything like me as adults, they will look back at my parenting critically and with copious and detailed notes of negative feedback.

Of course, what I want for my kids is for them to be emotionally healthy. That is the main goal. That is why I did all the research for this book.

But, if I'm being honest here, a secondary and perhaps less honorable wish is for them to also be grateful. I would love for my kids to one day tell a person researching how to raise twins, "You should talk to our mom." (Did I write *mom*? I meant *parents*.) "You should talk to our parents," they would say. And I would lower my head bashfully, blush, and say, "Aww, thanks. I don't know what to say." But inside my head would be an image of me doing a powerful yet awkward-looking victory dance.

Remember the proverb I highlighted in the introduction? Its edited form, adjusted for the modern age of parenting, is: "A loving and empathic parent understands what a child does not say." How can you be the most loving and empathic parent possible to your twin and non-twin children? Recognize that your twin children have a unique companionship while proactively relieving them from the burden of caretaker. Encourage them to be the beautiful individual human beings they are while refraining from comparing them to each other. Show that your love for your singleton is as strong as your love for your twins. Make a concerted effort to have special alone time with each child in your family. Think deeply about how your twins can best learn in an academic environment. Consider how twinship both expands and limits their abilities to make friends and find romantic partners. It is then that you can understand what your children may not be saying.

So that is my wish for you: be a loving and empathic parent. Be an excellent parent. Be a gold star parent. And if you do it right—and if the stars align—your kids may one day tell someone: "You should talk to my parents. They did it right." Just imagine.

1. Woody Allen and Marshall Brickman, *Annie Hall*, directed by Woody Allen (New York: United Artists, 1977).

2. "A Normal Day," YouTube video by Story of This Life, May 12, 2017, https://www.youtube.com/watch?v=bL7Y6S4dMjI.

3. Douglas Haddad, *The Ultimate Guide to Raising Teens and Tweens: Strategies for Unlocking Your Child's Full Potential* (Lanham, MA: Rowman & Littlefield, 2017).

4. Markham, *Aha! Parenting*.

5. Karyn Hall and Melissa Cook, *The Power of Validation: Arming Your Child against Bullying, Peer Pressure, Addiction, Self-Harm & Out-of-Control Emotions* (Oakland, CA: New Harbinger Publications, 2012).

# Bibliography

Allen, Woody, and Marshall Brickman. *Annie Hall.* Directed by Woody Allen. New York: United Artists, 1977.

"A Normal Day." YouTube video by Story of This Life, May 12, 2017. https://www.youtube.com/watch?v=bL7Y6S4dMjI.

Apter, Terri. *The Sister Knot: Why We Fight, Why We're Jealous, and Why We'll Love Each Other No Matter What.* New York: W. W. Norton & Company, 2007.

The BabyCenter Medical Advisory Board. "Your Likelihood of Having Twins or More." BabyCenter.com, last updated January 2016. https://www.babycenter.com/0_your-likelihood-of-having-twins-or-more_3575.bc#articlesection1.

Bingham, Mindy, and Sandy Stryker. *Things Will Be Different for My Daughter: A Practical Guide to Building Her Self-Esteem and Self-Reliance.* New York: Penguin, 1995.

Blas, Daniel. "Four's Company." *The Pennsylvania Gazette*, June 24, 2015. http://thepenngazette.com/fours-company/.

Bracken, Helmut von. "Mutual Intimacy in Twins: Types of Social Structure in Pairs of Identical and Fraternal Twins." *Journal of Personality* 2, no. 4 (1934): 293–309. 10.1111/j.1467-6494.1934.tb02106.x.

Brooks, Robert, and Sam Goldstein. *Raising Resilient Children: Fostering Strength, Hope, and Optimism in Your Child*. New York: McGraw-Hill, 2002.

Clinton, Bill. *My Life: The Early Years*. New York: Vintage Books, 2005.

Covey, Stephen. *The 7 Habits of Highly Effective Families*. New York: Golden Books, 1997.

Ebenbach, David H., and Dacher Keltner. "Power, Emotion, and Judgmental Accuracy in Social Conflict: Motivating the Cognitive Miser." *Basic and Applied Social Psychology* 20, no. 1 (1998): 7–21. http://dx.doi.org/10.1207/s15324834basp2001_2.

Eyre, Linda and Richard. *The Book of Nurturing: Nine Natural Laws for Enriching Your Family Life*. New York: McGraw-Hill, 2003.

Friedman, Joan. *Emotionally Healthy Twins: A New Philosophy for Parenting Two Unique Children*. Cambridge, MA: Da Capo Press, 2008.

Galinsky, Ellen. *Ask the Children: What America's Children Really Think about Working Parents*. New York: William Morrow and Company, 1999.

Haddad, Douglas. *The Ultimate Guide to Raising Teens and Tweens: Strategies for Unlocking Your Child's Full Potential*. Lanham, MA: Rowman & Littlefield, 2017.

Hall, Karyn D., and Melissa H. Cook. *The Power of Validation: Arming Your Child against Bullying, Peer Pressure, Addiction, Self-Harm & Out-of-Control Emotions*. Oakland, CA: New Harbinger Publications, 2012.

Hamilton, Brady E., Joyce A. Martin, Michelle J. K. Osterman, Sally C. Curtin, T. J. Mathews, and the National Center for Health Statistics. "Births: Final Data for 2014." *National Vital Statistics Reports* 64, no. 12 (December 23, 2015): 1–63. https://www.cdc.gov/nchs/data/nvsr/nvsr64/nvsr64_12.pdf.

Hart, Louise. *The Bullying Antidote: Superpower Your Kids for Life.* Center City, MN: Hazelden, 2013.

Kaplan Thaler, Linda, and Robin Koval. *Grit to Great: How Perseverance, Passion, and Pluck Take You from Ordinary to Extraordinary.* New York: Crown Business, 2015.

Kilner, Rebecca, Joah R. Madden, and Mark E. Hauber. "Brood Parasitic Cowbird Nestlings Use Host Young to Procure Resources." *Science* 305, no. 5685 (2004): 877–9. http://science.sciencemag.org/content/305/5685/877.

Kim, Eun Kyung. "Jenna Bush Hager, Sister Barbara Bush Share Secrets of Being a Twin." Today.com, June 22, 2015. https://www.today.com/health/jenna-bush-hager-sister-barbara-share-secrets-being-twins-t27756.

Kluger, Jeffrey. *The Sibling Effect: What the Bonds among Brothers and Sisters Reveal about Us.* New York: Riverhead Books, 2011.

Markham, Laura. "5 Strategies That Prevent Most Misbehavior." *Aha! Parenting,* August 4, 2016. http://www.ahaparenting.com/BlogRetrieve.aspx?PostID=469919&A=SearchResult&SearchID=10662406&ObjectID=469919&ObjectType=55.

McCready, Amy. *Positive Parenting Solutions.* Online webinar and blog: Positive Parenting Solutions, Inc., founded 2004. https://www.positiveparentingsolutions.com.

Mohr, Jay. *No Wonder My Parents Drank: Tales from a Stand-Up Dad*. New York: Simon & Schuster, 2010.

Perel, Esther, in an interview with Guy Raz. "Are We Asking Too Much of Our Spouses?" *National Public Radio*'s TED Radio Hour, April 25, 2014. http://www.npr.org/templates/transcript/transcript.php?storyId=301825600.

Pook, Lizzie. "'I've Never Needed Anyone Else': Life as an Identical Twin." *The Guardian*, October 29, 2016. https://www.theguardian.com/lifeandstyle/2016/oct/29/identical-twin-never-needed-anyone-else.

Senior, Jennifer. *All Joy and No Fun: The Paradox of Modern Parenthood*. New York: Ecco, 2015.

Sharrow, David J., and James J. Anderson. "A Twin Protection Effect? Explaining Twin Survival Advantages with a Two-Process Mortality Model." *PLoS ONE* 11, no. 5 (2016): e0154774. http://journals.plos.org/plosone/article/file?id=10.1371/journal.pone.0154774&type=printable

Singer, Tania, Ben Seymour, John P. O'Doherty, Klaas E. Stephan, Raymond J. Dolan, and Chris D. Frith. "Empathic Neural Responses Are Modulated by the Perceived Fairness of Others." *Nature* 439, no. 7075 (2006): 466–9. https://www.ncbi.nlm.nih.gov/pmc/articles/PMC2636868/pdf/ukmss-3669.pdf.

Spock, Benjamin. *The Common Sense Book of Baby and Child Care*. New York: Duell, Sloan and Pearce, 1946.

Zelizer, Viviana. *Pricing the Priceless Child: The Changing Social Value of Children*. Princeton, NJ: Basic Books, 1985.

# About the Author

DARA LOVITZ, Esq., graduated *magna cum laude* from the University of Pennsylvania and attended Temple University School of Law, where she won the Barrister Award. Lovitz is a continuing legal education project coordinator for the American Law Institute and an adjunct professor of Animal Law at Temple Law. She is a founding board member of the nonprofit organization Peace Advocacy Network.

Lovitz is the author of two previous books: *Muzzling a Movement: The Effects of Anti-Terrorism Laws, Money, and Politics on Animal Activism* (Lantern Books, 2010), and *Catching Falling Cradles: A Gentle Approach to Classic Rhymes* (self-published, 2014). The former title received the Top 10 Reads of 2010 award from the Institute of Critical Animal Studies and the 2010 Donut Award from the Vegan Police national podcast.

Lovitz's blog *Some Twinsight* is popular among parents of twins and she is gaining a growing following under her Twitter handle @TwinMomDara.

Lovitz becomes a passionate advocate for that which inspires her daily life. Before she became a mother, she dedicated all of her non-billable time to animal rights activism. After numerous conference presentations and television appearances, she developed a reputation for ardently providing a voice for the voiceless. When she became a parent, she transferred her need to protect those who cannot protect themselves to children. While she continues to apportion some of her time to animal activism, she has found a new motivator in life: being the best parent she can be. And, as with animal activism, she will seek to embolden others to join her in this endeavor.

# About Familius

## Visit Our Website: www.familius.com

## Join Our Family

There are lots of ways to connect with us! Subscribe to our newsletters at www.familius.com to receive uplifting daily inspiration, essays from our Pater Familius, a free ebook every month, and the first word on special discounts and Familius news.

## Get Bulk Discounts

If you feel a few friends and family might benefit from what you've read, let us know and we'll be happy to provide you with quantity discounts. Simply email us at orders@familius.com.

## Connect

- Facebook: www.facebook.com/paterfamilius
- Twitter: @familiustalk, @paterfamilius1
- Pinterest: www.pinterest.com/familius
- Instagram: @familiustalk

FAMILIUS

The most important work you ever do will be within the walls of your own home.

CPSIA information can be obtained
at www.ICGtesting.com
Printed in the USA
LVOW03s2337080218
565866LV00001B/2/P